PRAISE FOR *YOUR GUIDE TO PUBLIC SPEAKING*

"*Your Guide to Public Speaking* is a user-friendly book that introduces the core principles of public speaking in a way that anyone can pick up and implement. Drawing from real-world experience as a seasoned public speaking coach and actress, Amanda Hennessey does a superb job breaking down the art of good public speaking—which to many can be seen as a daunting, multifaceted, and complex topic—into actionable steps packaged in a practical, witty guide. Inspiring!"

—*Christie Lindor, TEDx speaker and author of the award-winning bestseller* The MECE Muse: 100+ Selected Practices, Unwritten Rules, and Habits of Great Consultants

"This book is nurturing, witty, and profoundly insightful. Amanda is that rare coach who offers a one-two punch—she is as smart as they come and writes straight from the heart. Her insider tips are not just essential to strong public speaking but to professional success!"

—*Alexandra Sullivan, cofounder of 44 Communications*

"Amanda approaches the art of speaking from a very unique and refreshing perspective—the deep root of why we speak and who we are as speakers. By focusing on our mission as speakers, on why we want to give the speech and the impact we will deliver to the audience, Amanda helps readers embrace speaking with love as the motivation. In her direct—yet fun and personable—style, Amanda guides readers to access their inner strengths and deeper selves, which enables them to bring more emotion and power to their delivery. This book offers a lot of fun and practical exercises that are refreshing and effective—no matter if you are just starting out or looking to reach higher goals in speaking."

—*Lei Wang, author, motivational speaker, and first Asian American to complete the Explorers Grand Slam (http://JourneywithLei.com)*

"Amanda is an authority on public speaking, and one of the most talented coaches I've met. It is mind-blowing to see how she makes public speaking—America's biggest phobia—not only much simpler but also a true source of self-empowerment for anyone. In this book, you will learn highly effective, easy-to-remember techniques that will help you become an authentic and confident public speaker. A must-read for those who want to have a bigger impact by empowering themselves and others."

—*Will G. Foussier, CEO and founder of Ace-up, Inc.*

"*Your Guide to Public Speaking* is a practical resource for new and experienced presenters alike. Amanda Hennessey walks the reader through every detail—from what to talk about, to how to harness nervous energy, to what to do with your hands during the presentation. The fundamental shift of focus from the presenter to the audience is the real game-changer. It reminded me that presentations are really all about making a connection with the people in the room."

—*Maura Herson, assistant dean of MIT Sloan School MBA Program*

"I am so happy the world finally gets to share in Amanda's extremely practical, user-friendly, and unique approach to preparing for public speaking. She has a true gift of understanding people and helping them open up and find their authentic selves, and she conveys this in a kind and supportive manner. As a dog trainer who teaches group classes and has periodic media appearances and interviews, I refer to this manual as an invaluable reminder to stay focused and on track with my training message. It's a must-have book for all!"

—*Kate Perry of Kate Perry Dog Training, named New York's Best Dog Trainer by New York magazine*

"Like a great play, a great speech is based in storytelling. Amanda's background in the theater endows this book with personal and emotional insights that move it beyond an old-fashioned public speaking text into a fresh, creative approach for our technology-driven time. She offers clear, easy-to-use techniques to empower the speaker and awaken passion, authenticity, and the value of being 'fully present.' All of this good advice is presented with a sensitivity to the natural fears and perceptual obstacles that even the best speakers confront. By directly addressing the physical, vocal, and mental dimensions of public speaking, she provides a detailed, practical, and inspirational guide that is sure to transform your presentation and engage your audience—while also awakening your best self."

—*Scott Edmiston, Elliot Norton Award–winning theater director, professor of the practice, Northeastern University*

"Much like that favorite teacher from childhood who seemed to have only one objective in mind—to unconditionally share everything she knows with you—Amanda Hennessey shares her knowledge about public speaking gained over the years. *Your Guide to Public Speaking* enables us to prepare ourselves mentally, emotionally, and content-wise, and provides us with an actual process of conveying that content to an audience in a format that is impactful. By being passionate, confident, and prepared, you will be able to take your audience on a journey where it learns deeply about something you know and care about."

—*Imac Maria Zambrana, associate professor, faculty of educational sciences, University of Oslo*

YOUR GUIDE TO
PUBLIC
SPEAKING

Build Your Confidence, Find Your Voice, and INSPIRE YOUR AUDIENCE

AMANDA HENNESSEY

Adams Media

New York   London   Toronto   Sydney   New Delhi

This book is dedicated to those who have a
positive message and don't know how to share it.
And to those who have not yet found their voice.

Adams Media
An Imprint of Simon & Schuster, Inc.
57 Littlefield Street
Avon, Massachusetts 02322

First Adams Media trade paperback edition
May 2019

ADAMS MEDIA and colophon are
trademarks of Simon & Schuster.

For information about special discounts
for bulk purchases, please contact Simon &
Schuster Special Sales at 1-866-506-1949 or
business@simonandschuster.com.

The Simon & Schuster Speakers Bureau can
bring authors to your live event. For more
information or to book an event contact
the Simon & Schuster Speakers Bureau at
1-866-248-3049 or visit our website at
www.simonspeakers.com.

Interior design by Julia Jacintho
Interior images © Getty Images/iconeer

Manufactured in the United States
of America

10 9 8 7 6 5 4 3 2

Library of Congress Cataloging-in-
Publication Data
Names: Hennessey, Amanda, author.
Title: Your guide to public speaking /
Amanda Hennessey.
Description: Avon, Massachusetts: Adams
Media, 2019.
Includes index.
Identifiers: LCCN 2018056697 |
ISBN 9781507210246 (pb) |
ISBN 9781507210253 (ebook)
Subjects: LCSH: Public speaking.
Classification: LCC PN4129.15 .H465 2019 |
DDC 808.5/1--dc23
LC record available at
https://lccn.loc.gov/2018056697

ISBN 978-1-5072-1024-6
ISBN 978-1-5072-1025-3 (ebook)

CONTENTS

CHAPTER 3

CHAPTER 4

PART THREE | The Presentation   117

CHAPTER 5

CHAPTER 6

CHAPTER 7

INTRODUCTION

Many of my clients describe their experience of public speaking like a horror movie: heart-racing dread, vivid nightmares, an intense desperation to escape, and a fear of being destroyed.

Yikes!

Believe it or not, the experience of preparing and presenting does not need to torment you as though you were a babysitter hearing creepy noises in the basement. It can be a swashbuckling adventure into the unknown, complete with a mission, discovery, passion, and rewards. Instead of heart-racing dread, you can have heart-racing excitement, along with epic storytelling; humor; total engagement of heart, body, and soul; and an urgent sense of purpose motivating you! Not only can it feel as if you are in an adventure movie, but the content of your speech can also be so much better. It can be powerful, memorable, and make an impact.

Everyone has to speak in front of an audience at some point, whether in a personal or professional capacity. The ability to capture and keep an audience's attention is a powerful skill, and it doesn't have to be one you're born with. *Your Guide to Public Speaking* will help you learn, practice, and improve, regardless of your current degree of competency.

No matter what you are asked to present (a proposal at work or a wedding toast) or who's asking you to speak (your boss or your best friend), you want to be able to engage the task with confidence and enthusiasm. If you've never received any kind of training on how to approach public speaking or how to dynamically share your message with an audience, you're not alone.

I've been coaching and leading public speaking workshops for people from many different industries for more than a decade. I know how lost and overwhelmed many people feel. I've also witnessed my clients evolve beautifully and grow their confidence, skills, and courage. In this book I'll share a variety of strategies and tools for establishing a positive mindset, using your voice effectively, and shaping the content of your speech thoughtfully.

Whether you struggle with mindset, metaphors, monotone, or what to do with your hands, this easy-to-read guide will set you on the path toward public speaking success. Presenting with excellence requires you to stay continually present in each moment. This book will outline how to cultivate the art of staying present, which leads to that magic ingredient —presence. You will learn how to own your talk and own the floor. Whether you are speaking at a large conference, in a small internal meeting, at a lecture hall, on a conference or video call, at a wedding hall, or on a podcast, you will understand how to command your arena while still going with the flow.

Your Guide to Public Speaking will coach you on how to create an engaging journey for your audience so that they leave the experience changed in some way. Perhaps they will want to fund your project, choose to join your cause, or see the world differently. You can achieve these goals and more when you authentically and passionately share your message with an audience…and enjoy doing it!

PART ONE

Public Speaking 101

Every week I receive emails from people who are stressed out and really struggling as they prepare for a presentation. They feel overwhelmed and ill-equipped to get up in front of a group, big or small, and talk. Here's an example of a typical email I find in my inbox:

"I struggle with confidence and my nerves feel out of control. I know I'm going to have to present in grad school, and I don't know how I am going to handle it. Help!"

If you were the sender of this email and we scheduled a coaching session, the first thing we would address is your relationship with the experience of public speaking. This complex relationship has many components:

- **Your relationship with what the experience is about**—Is your focus to not screw up? Is it about proving something? Is it about giving something of value to the audience?
- **Your relationship with your nervous system**—Do you think feeling nervous is a terrible thing? Do you believe that if you have nerves, your presentation can still be a success? Are you nervous about being nervous?
- **Your relationship with yourself**—Are incredibly high standards of perfection freezing you in your tracks? Are you very self-critical (which gets in the way of a healthy and creative process)?
- **Your relationship with the audience**—Do you want to "get it over with" to escape being the center of attention? Can you imagine being present moment to moment with your audience?

We're going to examine these relationships in Part One. They are the foundation of excellence in public speaking, so they're the best place to start.

CHAPTER 1

What Is Public Speaking?

The term *public speaking* encompasses many types of presentations, events, and audiences. In this chapter we'll talk about some of those, and then move on to discovering your personal perspective on talking to a group. You'll discover the benefits of wanting to present rather than "having to," and how your mindset makes a huge difference. You'll also learn how to avoid the pitfalls of perfectionism. Yes, I want you to deeply care about your skills, your mission, your slides, and your audience, but I don't want you to be racked with worry about what the audience may think of you.

Public Speaking, Defined

Public speaking is a broad term that describes many different scenarios that share a common thread: you are sharing ideas with a group. Public speaking includes anything from a TED Talk to a toast at a wedding and everything in between. If the phrase *public speaking* freaks you out, then substitute the phrases *sharing ideas* or *having a conversation* or think of it like *talking with people—authentically, from the heart, soul, and brain—for a specific purpose.*

The group may be large, as in a graduation ceremony or an awards reception. But often your audience will be smaller. Here are other common public speaking opportunities you might encounter:

- Speaking during a team meeting at work
- Leading (or contributing to) a weekly conference call or webinar, perhaps via a video conferencing application, such as Zoom or Skype
- Presenting a research poster at a conference
- Demonstrating a product on a trade show floor
- Participating in a Q&A after your film premiere
- Sitting on a panel, publicly sharing your expertise in some area
- Asking a question at a public forum or meeting
- Pitching a product or idea in front of a group
- Recording your own podcast or *YouTube* videos

Regardless of where your audience is (in the room with you or halfway across the world), the subject matter (Habitat for Humanity or nuclear physics), or the forum (your child's school or a city arena), public speaking is simply people conveying their thoughts to a group.

Why People Speak Publicly

There are many different reasons why people talk to an audience. You may want (or be asked) to educate, inspire, entertain, explain, chastise, defend, or encourage. Being a compelling communicator can open doors for you and others. You can:

- Advance causes you care about
- Make urgently needed changes in systems, government, and society
- Help and encourage others
- Motivate teams that are disheartened
- Inspire and entertain people who desperately need to laugh and find their inner strength rather than cry and give up

You might be speaking because:

- Your boss is pushing you to grow and have greater visibility within your organization. She may see you as a potential leader with fresh new ideas that will give the team a new perspective.
- Your friend has chosen you to give a wedding toast because you know him really well and have weathered the ups and downs of life with him.
- An organization you volunteer for has asked you to speak about your personal experiences to inspire others to donate their money and time.
- Your friend has invited you to be a guest on her podcast because you are funny and an expert on a topic the show is covering.
- Your high school has asked you to speak to seniors about your college experience so they can know what to look forward to and what challenges to prepare for.

Think of an invitation or requirement to speak publicly as a great opportunity to be heard and seen. You have the potential to affect people in a positive way and challenge yourself to build your confidence, knowledge, and influence.

If you're not sure why you are speaking, chances are you can figure it out if you contemplate it for a few minutes. A specific message needs to be given to a specific group of people. Apparently an email, text, tweet, or video is not going to cut it. A real, live person is the best choice for communicating the ideas, stories, and/or call to action.

The Main Reason: The Audience Needs You

Notice that in the examples I just gave, I put the emphasis on the positive impact you can have on *others* by speaking. I'm not immediately focusing on how you'll get lots of praise from your boss, coworkers, professor, or *YouTube* followers. Yes, it is awesome when your boss tells you that you did an excellent job, your coworkers give you a high five, and your followers comment that you nailed it. Yes, I want you to thrive in your career and endeavors, progress in your development, and make your fortune—of course! I want you to be empowered. It's great to be encouraged and validated by other people's feedback. But I have found in all of my years as a coach that gaining the approval of others is not the most helpful or empowering motivator for being a great public speaker.

> *"The way you overcome shyness is to become so wrapped up in something that you forget to be afraid."*
> —Lady Bird Johnson

When you step back and think deeply about *why* you are speaking to a group about a particular topic, you will be less stressed if you do not make it all about you, your status, your image, and your reputation. If you get fired up about the impact you can make, your passion will be your fuel.

The next time you are told you will need to speak publicly, examine the context and figure out what your audience needs. They may need training, they may need inspiration, or they may need a wake-up call.

You will have more courage and charisma when you are grounded in this way. Rather than trying to get something *from* your audience, you will be concerned with creating a compelling experience *for* them. After all, you are there to give a talk or presentation, not to get one. Be generous as you give.

What's Your Perspective on Public Speaking?

When you think about having to speak publicly, what feelings or emotions arise for you? Fear appears to be the default, the norm. In fact, many articles, studies, and polls report that people are more afraid of public speaking than they are of death!

Feeling Resistant?

Feeling forced or obligated to do something you don't want to do is not fun or empowering. Resistance and other negative feelings arise and can block your creativity and confidence. If you are freaked out and annoyed that you have to present, change your perspective. You've got to do it, so why not make the most of the experience?

What if we could change this general impression of doom and gloom? We can—by shifting our perspective on public speaking from one driven by fear to one motivated by love. It might feel silly at first to talk about love in this context, but it speaks to how personal and special the task of public speaking really is. Focusing on what you love about the topic or situation will go a long way in switching your driving force from fear to love. Being motivated by love feels better, yields better results, and is more powerful in the end. Whether you are presenting a report on the two-toed sloth, asking for $5,000 contributions at a fundraiser, or saying your wedding vows, you can let love guide you or fear control you.

It's up to you.

Activity: Set Yourself Up for Success

The following exercise will help you frame your upcoming experience in ways that set you up for success rather than stress you out.

1. Think about an upcoming presentation. (If you do not have a specific one coming up, imagine one that could potentially come your way at a future time.) What do you need to do? (Examples: I need to present research in class, I need to contribute to a team meeting at work, I need to write a toast for my cousin's wedding.)

2. What is the purpose of your mission? What do you want the audience to get out of what you are sharing? (Do you want them to learn something or change their thinking? Do you want them to be inspired, encouraged, and/or entertained? Do you want them to take action?)

3. Do you want to give the speech? Why or why not?

If you said that you don't really want to speak about this topic, are your reasons based on your own fears or based on the subject of the talk? (For example: I don't mind speaking; I just think my cousin is making a terrible mistake marrying this dude and I want no part of it!)

Teasing out the goal of your presentation and any fears you have surrounding it will often help you see more clearly any obstacles that could get in the way of your success. Remembering your passion before you begin writing content and facing your fears right off the bat will make the whole process go more smoothly.

Knowing What's at Stake for Your Audience

One of the ways you can put a public speaking event into perspective is to think about what is at stake for your audience. What do they have to gain or lose based on what you say? Your job as a public speaker is to be very clear on why what you are saying is important. Investing yourself fully in the stakes of your mission will help you gain the attention and respect of your audience. And it will help to remind you that it's not about you.

Are There Always Stakes?

You may be wondering if there are some instances where there aren't stakes for the audience, such as in the case of a toast at a wedding. Nope—there is always something at stake. If you are giving a maid-of-honor speech, your primary audience, the couple, either will get to hear from you about your support and love for them or they will not. That is what is at stake.

In his book, *The Actor and the Target*, film and stage director Declan Donnellan discusses why, for a production to be successful, it is essential that the stakes are higher for the character than they are for the actor playing that character. (In a nutshell, the show will be amazing if the actress playing Juliet keeps her full focus on her relationship with

Romeo, rather than worrying what the prestigious agent in the fourth row is thinking about her.) The same can be said for a successful presentation. It is essential that the stakes are higher regarding the goal or message than they are for the presenter.

When the Stakes Are Personal

Sometimes there are a few things at stake. I had a client tell me, "My boss told me that I won't be promoted unless my next presentation on our new cyber security system goes really well." This is very important information, and potentially what motivated the person to seek out coaching with me. But it doesn't change the fact that the *audience* needs to be your main focus.

Imagine if you were this person. Here are your personal stakes: you could gain a promotion or lose a promotion. You could gain or lose the respect of your boss. You could get a raise or not. These stakes are high. They are also incredibly nerve-racking. This perspective has the potential to turn your entire focus toward you. This will feel terrible and distract from the stakes that are actually helpful and crucial for success.

You will have such a better chance of giving a winning performance if, instead, you focus on what is at stake for your audience. If they take action, what will be gained? If action is not taken, what will be lost? In regard to the cyber security presentation, you could paint a crystal-clear picture of what the potential client stands to lose if they do not invest in a state-of-the-art security system. Then you can share all they will gain by purchasing your company's service. In so doing, you are helping them to understand what is at stake—for them. If you get bogged down by your personal stakes of worrying about a promotion, you are likely to be insecure, anxious, and self-conscious. And this state will not serve anyone in the room.

Knowing the Stakes Can Help You Ignite Passion

Imagine you work for a social service agency and the area you live in is expecting a rare heat wave. At tomorrow's town hall meeting it is your job to remind your community of the dangers of leaving kids and pets in the car in such extreme heat. It's also critical that people check in on elderly relatives and neighbors. What is at stake? The lives of children, the elderly, and animals. If people don't listen and take action, lives could be lost. If the audience does listen, lives can be protected. If you become invested in the audience's stakes in this scenario, your passion will be ignited and you will want to be seen and heard by everyone in the room.

Real-World Example:
A Management Consultant Shifts Her Perspective

Many people can lose sight of what's most important for their public speaking engagements when they could be personally affected by their performance. The following example shows how refocusing on the audience can lead to better results.

Gabrielle, a management consultant at a *Fortune* 500 company, was asked to lead a webinar on best practices for project managers. Not only would there be many project managers tuning in to the lesson, but a number of senior managers would also be logged on. Gabrielle was a go-getter who loved a challenge. She had a lot of wisdom to share about how to be an excellent project manager, but this was information she had shared many times before, so it didn't feel like an exciting challenge. Gabrielle also wanted to make a great impression on senior management, which made her stressed.

I wanted to help Gabrielle shift gears so that she could step into her sweet spot—inspiring others to think differently and take better actions. I asked if the project managers wanted this training. She shared that they really did. Many of them were feeling overwhelmed and stressed. They needed new strategies pronto! I said, "Picture all of the people who are potentially affected by these project managers' competency or lack thereof: all of their coworkers, any clients they interact with, their spouses, their kids, even their pets. There could be a lot of anxiety and pain stemming from a single project manager's insecurity about their ability to do their job. And you can relieve this! You may not see them visually because you are on a webinar, but you can picture women and men who are freaking out and fortunately, really open to help, surrounded by others who want them to get that help. Your tall glass of wisdom will be so valuable to these really thirsty people in the desert."

As I spoke I could see Gabrielle getting more invested and excited about making an impact. She knew she could give people the guidance and strategies they needed to thrive. As we rehearsed, she became more focused, passionate, and present, and she really sounded like she was on her listeners' team. Her worries about what senior management would think of her dissipated. Now that Gabrielle was fully engaged in her mission, there wasn't time or headspace to be distracted by the presence of senior management. The webinar was no longer about her, which was incredibly freeing.

She nailed it!

The Problem with Perfection

Often, during a first session, clients tell me that their presentation has to be *perfect*. I ask them to describe what their perfect public speaking experience would be like. They might say something like, "I'm calm and relaxed. I don't stumble over any words. People take me seriously and laugh when I want them to. My slides cooperate. Everyone loves my talk and thinks I am a great speaker."

> ## From Crying to Coaching
>
> A woman shared with me that when she was eighteen years old, she got up in class to speak, freaked out, and left the room in tears. Years later she became a teaching assistant for undergrads in engineering and coached students on how to present powerfully. At the final presentations, professors in the department commented that these were the best presentations they'd seen in years. There's no reason to let an embarrassing experience define and limit you—just learn from your past and move forward!

While these are worthy goals, you can see that their focus is on themselves and not the audience and what *they* need. By turning their attention inward, they are putting a lot of pressure on themselves to meet these high expectations. Unfortunately, attempting to be perfect is only going to frustrate and distract them. Another problematic issue is that the definition of perfection is very subjective! You might hear people say that you did a great job, but you feel like you bombed.

The word *perfect* can make you feel that you are walking on a tightrope, terrified of making a mistake, and that's not the mindset you want when you're speaking. Let it go. Strive for excellence instead. Aim to prepare yourself as completely as possible and then do the best job you can. Sure, a slide might be glitchy, but that doesn't mean the audience didn't get your message. If you keep the stakes for the audience in mind at all times, you'll see how quickly perfection becomes less important. You'll instead find yourself focused on making sure the audience gets the information they need, and you'll realize that you don't have to be perfect to get your message across.

Don't Miss Out

Some of my older clients tell me that their avoidance of public speaking has cost them career advancement, salary increases, and opportunities to make an impact. In some cases their fears have prevented them from feeling comfortable in social settings and family events. Face your fears head-on so you don't miss out!

The Process Won't Be Perfect Either— and That's Okay!

The process of preparing a speech probably isn't going to be perfect either. Preparing for your experience is a process in and of itself, and it's filled with smaller processes: writing the talk, putting together a slide deck, practicing aloud. Each of these creative processes is covered in this book (see Chapter 5).

The word *perfect* will not be your friend for any of these phases of your project. Are you picturing that each word you type will be exactly the right word? Do you imagine that your first draft will be your final draft? Will your first go at your slides perfectly illustrate what you are trying to express? Nope—*all* of these components will require editing, revisions, and redos.

Have you ever seen one of those home makeover shows? We witness many steps during an episode—brainstorming, planning, demolition, building, and staging. The house becomes a chaotic mess before it is transformed into a masterpiece. It is a necessary and perfectly messy process from start to finish.

The processes for creating your presentation will also be perfectly messy. You will write sentences and outlines, edit them, delete them, resurrect them, and so on. Your table and sofa may get covered in drafts, half-eaten bags of popcorn, and empty cans of Red Bull as you work on your talk or pitch.

You may have an initial vision of what your final presentation will look like…and then inspiration strikes in the midst of your process and nudges you to approach things in a different way. If you are too attached to that "perfect" vision that you originally came up with and ignore the new ideas that are flowing, you may miss out on some truly innovative concepts that come your way as you create. Forget perfection and focus on excellence and doing the best job you can.

Real-World Example:
Joshua Prepares for Medical School Interviews

Preparing for interviews can be nerve-racking, and perfectionism may rear its ugly head if you fear you won't get the position or placement if you aren't perfect. In the following story you'll learn about Joshua, who shifted away from his unhelpful perfectionism.

Joshua was preparing for his interviews for medical school. During our first session he showed me questions interviewers might ask as well as his detailed responses. His drive and intelligence were abundantly clear. But so was the pressure he was putting on himself to be perfect. I could see the tension in his body and sense his emotional distress.

Joshua had already memorized his answers, which unfortunately made them sound overly rehearsed. I could see that if he loosened up, his responses would become more conversational. More of his personality would come through and the interviewers would not only learn about his accomplishments, goals, and dreams, but would also get to know him. This would make Joshua a more memorable candidate.

I encouraged him to adjust his body language to let go of the physical tension he was carrying. He shifted the way he was sitting from a rigid, tight, constrained posture to one that was more expansive and relaxed but still alert. This change grounded him and enabled him to exude more confidence and breathe easier. (Chapter 3 will delve deeply into the important subject of body language.)

His initial strategy—hoping to say the exact right answer in the exact right way to get the interviewer to approve of him—was not setting him up for success. So, Joshua shifted his perspective. He began viewing interviews as opportunities for interviewers to learn about his authentic and long-held passion for medicine, his goals, and his growth as a student and person. Sharing with intelligence, honesty, some humility, and humor was a much more rewarding and effective option than grasping for so-called perfect answers.

Over time Joshua's answers no longer sounded overly rehearsed; they sounded spontaneous and had a lot of vocal variety. (More on this subject in Chapter 4.) Ultimately, his discipline and determination to be himself at his interviews paid off when he was accepted by a top-notch medical school.

Activity: Learn from Your Past Experience

Public speaking, at its core, is sharing ideas with a group (big or small) for a reason. Keeping this definition in mind, take a moment to remember times when you've spoken in public before. Make a list of these experiences, small and large.

Look at that—you've done this before and survived! It may have been messier or more awkward than you wanted, but that's okay. Please be kind to yourself as you look at your list so you can appreciate what you achieved and also learn from your past experiences. Go through each experience and answer the following questions for each one:

- What was at stake for you?
- What was at stake for your audience?
- When relevant, what happened if people took action after you shared with them?
- What happened if they did not take action?
- What is the most empowering motivation you can think of for each past experience (that is not about you or your personal stakes)?

This list should give you a good sense of where you stand now—the successes you've enjoyed, and those that you think had room for improvement. Maybe you were too focused on your personal stakes and lost sight of your passion for the topic. Maybe you over-prepared and sounded too robotic, or maybe you waited till the last minute and forgot key points. These are common mistakes, and ones we'll address throughout this book. Use this list to remind yourself of both your strengths and the areas you can develop, adjust, and improve.

PART TWO

The Presenter

Confidence is a key part of public speaking. Many people want to develop more confidence but aren't sure how to do it. This part will give you many tools and strategies for feeling ready and excited to be seen and heard. Chapter 2 will explore how to increase your confidence on an emotional and mental level, and Chapter 3 will cover how your body language choices can shift your outlook and bolster your confidence. Developing your voice in regard to breathing, projection, and vocal variety will be addressed in Chapter 4. These elements will allow you to more creatively express your ideas. You'll also learn how to leave distracting filler words, such as *um* and *like*, at home.

CHAPTER 2

Empowering Yourself Emotionally and Mentally

This chapter will help you create a strong emotional and mental foundation for your public speaking experiences. I will address topics that many people have concerns about: confidence, nerves, and being the center of attention. I will spend time exploring belief systems, so that you can determine which of your beliefs are setting you up to succeed and which ones are undermining your confidence and resilience. Presence and being present in the moment are both critical aspects of making an impact; I'll discuss these concepts and you will learn how they relate to one another.

Confidence

There are many components that work together to create confident public speakers. In this context confidence is made up of:

- Conviction in the points you are trying to make with your talk, presentation, pitch, or toast. The more you value your message and its possible impact, and the more passionate about it you are, the more confident you will become.
- The skills you need to approach the tasks of brainstorming, writing, rehearsing, and presenting.
- The ability/adaptability to handle the unknowns that appear along the way.

This chapter will unpack concepts to help you build your confidence. All of the strategies in this book, whether they are about body language, slides, or clichés, will increase your skill set and knowledge, giving you the confidence that you have the tools you need to prepare and speak publicly.

Who Are You?

A lack of self-confidence often appears as a questioning of your very being, such as:

- Who am I to get up in front of this crowd?
- Who am I to lead this meeting?
- Who am I to give my opinion?
- Who am I to apply for this job?

If you have ever asked yourself these questions, then you have experienced how disempowering they are. These questions have judgment baked into them and can lead you to feeling small. To build confidence, turn the "Who am I?" question on its head. Instead, list all of the reasons you *are* the person to take on the challenge at hand.

Here are some statements to consider:

- I have experience in this area.
- I have given this topic a lot of time and attention.
- I have a different or unusual perspective on this subject matter.
- My background in several different areas enables me to see this from a new angle.

Here are some additional statements that could bolster your confidence:

- I'm willing to learn.
- I'm willing to seek out the support I need to do the job well.
- I'm willing to push myself and grow.

I had a light-bulb moment about the "Who am I?" question during a conversation with a mentor. Feeling overwhelmed, I said to her, "Who am I to be taking on this task?" She lovingly challenged me. "Tell me, who are you? Who are you to be doing this?"

I took a few moments to mull it over and then answered with a list of grounded reasons as to why I was qualified to handle what was in front of me. I didn't become a raving egomaniac, but I suddenly felt very equipped to face the task at hand. This whole process took about two to four minutes and led to a powerful shift for me. Earlier the smallest part of myself had asked that question out of fear, insecurity, inferiority, and overwhelm. In contrast, the biggest part of me answered the question from a place of strength, wisdom, self-knowledge, and love.

Activity: List and Appreciate Your Qualifications

Here are beginnings of statements that can lead you to some helpful new ways to think about your qualifications for speaking about a specific topic. Jot down what comes to mind as you read them.

- I know a lot about _____ .

- When I experienced _____ ,

  I learned _____ .

- I am concerned about _____ .

- I am hopeful about _____ .

Reminding yourself about your skills and qualifications is a great way to build your confidence. Revisit this exercise periodically so you always have an updated list.

Get Emotionally Centered by Focusing On Your Mission

Instead of focusing on nerves or potential technological snafus, direct your emotional energy toward the ideas you are trying to communicate, why they matter, and what is at stake. Here are some questions that can help you to tap into your passion as you gain clarity on your mission.

- What needs to change in your organization, society, or the world?
- Why does this change matter?
- Who is affected negatively or positively by the way things currently are?

- Who will benefit if the change you are championing happens?
- Why is this change important to you?

The more you are personally and passionately invested in your mission, the more powerful your emotions will be, and the more effective and confident your communication will be.

Presence, Presenting, and Being Present

A key part of successful presenting is staying present. Being present is being mindfully aware of yourself and your environment in the moment. When you are fully present while sharing your talk, you are much more likely to take your audience on a journey with you moment by moment.

We've all seen performers and speakers with stage presence. They engage us and we can't take our eyes off of them. They may be highly entertaining, deeply serious, or somewhere in between.

If you are present, you present better! When you are present, you develop presence. When you have presence, people watch and listen to you. The present is the most powerful place to be—you will not find solid ground if you are trying to live in the past or future. What does that mean in the context of public speaking? You need to find a way to enjoy your time onstage.

Here's the tricky thing: often, in the beginning, we don't actually *want* to be present with our audiences. We do not want to be onstage, we do not want to be the center of attention, and we do not really want to be seen or heard. Invisibility is much more preferable, because it feels mentally and physically safer. We just want to get it over with as fast as possible, as though we were getting inoculations at the doctor's office. We want to do exactly what we did in rehearsal (if we had one): when the stakes felt lower, we read our slides word for word, and we quickly get off the stage. If we could we would outsource this terrifying task in a (pounding) heartbeat. In short, we're either trying to live in the past, reliving our practice runs, or jumping ahead to the future, when this presentation will be over!

Feeling Burned Out?

If you are feeling burned out, it can be harder to tap into passion for your message. Take a break and step back in order to see the bigger picture. Remind yourself why you are doing what you do. Also, take a moment to write down your accomplishments thus far.

Read the following three sentences aloud and note the differences among them.

1. Today, I want to talk at you about…
2. Today, I want to talk to you about…
3. Today, I want to talk with you about…

Which one of these sentences feels the most intimate? Which implies a sense of give-and-take between you and the audience?

When I think of the first sentence, I envision hurling ideas and thoughts at the audience, hoping they will catch what I am throwing. That sounds rough.

When I consider the second sentence, I get a sense that I will be looking my audience members in the eye as I speak to them. That's better but still feels one-sided.

When I contemplate the third sentence, I envision treating the audience with respect and wanting to engage with them. There may be some kind of exchange between us. I feel more open and present when I consider being with my audience. My defenses go down. We are in this experience together. This mindset is where the magic happens.

When you speak *with* your audience, you guide them through an experience. You are present with them, moment to moment. You develop presence when you are present while presenting. Let that be your goal (and maybe also the tongue twister you use to warm up backstage).

Activity: Practicing Presence

Just like any other skill, it takes practice to develop stage presence. This exercise will help you zero in on times in your life when you were truly living in the moment so you can remember the feeling.

1. List several times in the past few years when you have felt totally alive and in the moment. Maybe you were engaging in a sport or activity you love, laughing with your best friend, or sharing a unique experience with someone you care about.
2. Describe what each experience felt like. List your top emotions at the time.
3. Which feelings are similar?
4. Where was your focus during each event?

Believe it or not, you can have these same feelings when you are presenting. You can be in the moment, free from self-consciousness. The following part of this exercise will help you to be present, right now.

1. Take a deep breath and observe and contemplate things that are happening outside of you in this moment. Don't worry about writing anything down. Just observe. What are the sounds in the room? Where is the light coming in? Are there any shadows? Heighten your awareness of your breathing and take note of the movement of the air in your body.

2. Look at an object in the room. Really look at it. Be curious about all elements of it. If negative thoughts come up (like *This is stupid. I don't want to do this. What's the point? When is she going to tell me what to do with my hands?*), calmly recognize them and try to move past them and keep examining the object. Allow the distracting snarkiness to fade into the background as you focus more on the object than on the negative thoughts. (Don't worry; I'll cover what to do with your hands in Chapter 3.) Take a breath. Consider the object's shape, color, texture, weight, and purpose.

3. In those moments of being fully present with the object, what are your physical, mental, and emotional experiences?

Taking an improv or an acting class can be another great way to learn how to be present in the moment and other awesome performance strategies.

How to Get Out of Your Own Way

One of the main challenges of preparing yourself mentally and emotionally is to stop focusing on the negative (nerves, potential problems) or on misguided assumptions you have. Let's look closer at these unhelpful thoughts.

Mistake #1: Thinking You Should Be Calm Onstage

You probably think you want to be calm onstage, right? But think a little harder about that. Will being super chill and calm while presenting make the impact you want? Did you ever leave a riveting speech or performance and say, "Wow, I was so moved. That performer was so calm"?

"Beyoncé blew me away! She was so relaxed." "The amazing speaker at that rally was so chill."

I'm guessing no. What gets and keeps our attention is a performance that is electric, dynamic, and passionate rather than calm, contained, and controlled...more along the lines of, "That performer was a force of nature! She was on fire!" "His speech was awesome. He was so alive!"

These words all imply that there is a lot of energy on the stage or set. When people use energy driven by passion and purpose, that's what lights up a stage. The more committed and passionate you are about the topic at hand, the more riveting you will be. So instead of thinking you need to be super chill, spend some time determining what the best amount of energy is for your particular event.

Mistake #2: Thinking That Feeling Nervous Is a Bad Thing

You might think, *I wish I didn't feel so nervous—this pit in my stomach, my heart racing, and my hands and voice shaking. These butterflies are killing me! How do I stop this madness? I feel terrible and am really distracted.*

Let's break this down. There are the physical responses you are having: a rapid heartbeat, sweating, or shaky hands. And then there are the thoughts, usually judgments, you are having about these responses: *This feels awful! Everyone can see I'm a wreck! My body is being taken over by stress and I can't think straight! Get me out of here!*

What's happening is that you are nervous about being nervous. These thoughts do not help you focus, nor does this narrative set you up to succeed. Accepting these physical responses, rather than judging them and making up stories about what they mean, is key. The more comfortable you can get with the reactions of your body, the less stressed you will be. Instead of reacting with panic to shaky hands and a racing heart, see if you can respond with acceptance and patience. Check out these reactions:

- *My hands are shaking. It's okay. That's all right. It just means I've got some extra energy flowing through my body, which I actually really need right now!*
- *My heart is racing. It's okay. I'm going to take a deep breath and slow down. The issue I'm sharing with my audience deeply matters to me, so it makes sense that I feel a reaction when I think about it.*

Of course, if you fear that you are having a medical emergency, seek medical attention immediately.

But in all other circumstances accepting how you feel is much better than fighting how you feel. Acknowledge what is happening, but do all you can to refrain from making up a negative horror story. See if you can observe the thoughts and connect them to a positive thing rather than taking them down a negative path. Be sure to also reassure yourself that you are okay.

Would you judge Martin Luther King Jr. if his hands had been shaking during his incredibly powerful "I Have a Dream" speech? If your favorite singer was sweating when she was belting out a song, would you like the song less? That's how you can reassure yourself that nerves won't affect your message unless you let them. Butterflies are beautiful and mesmerizing. They are not your enemy!

Activity: Your Relationship with Your Nerves

Thinking about your nerves objectively is a good way to separate them from the content of your presentation. As you answer the following questions, not only will you heighten your awareness of your current responses to your nerves, but you'll also create some new strategies to try.

1. If you are nervous, what happens to you physically? (Examples: I feel like I have butterflies in my stomach, I turn bright red, I start to sweat, I feel the adrenaline.)
2. If you are nervous, what happens to you mentally? (Examples: I go blank, my thoughts race, I get very self-critical, I get really focused.)
3. If you are nervous, what happens to you emotionally? (Examples: I get emotional, I'm scared everyone can see I'm nervous, I feel like a failure, I feel good, I am challenging myself in a new way.)
4. Is a need to be perfect or a fear of being imperfect part of why you feel nervous?

Now that you have an outline of how you've felt about your nerves in the past, you can identify areas that could use improvement in the future. The following questions will give you new strategies for the next time you feel nervous.

1. What could be a healthy way to think about striving for excellence and being the best version of yourself?
2. The next time you are having the physical experiences you described in response to the first question, what are some helpful ways for you to talk to yourself about them?

Tips for Effective Emotional and Mental Preparation

Here are some elements to consider integrating into your prep time if possible. They can help you feel calmer or more energized, depending on what you need at the moment.

- **Surround yourself with positive energy.** When you are feeling overwhelmed or defeated, emotional support from caring and encouraging friends, family, and colleagues will help buoy your spirits and get you back on track.
- **Ask for help.** Intellectual and creative support from trusted friends, family, and colleagues can make obstacles easier to overcome and tricky subjects simpler to master.
- **Get regular exercise.** Exercise is a great stress reliever! Vigorous exercise is helpful for releasing tension and endorphins (chemicals that trigger feelings that are positive). Options like yoga and Pilates are great for breathing, concentration, strength, and meditation. Walks in nature can be calming as well.
- **Take breaks.** Just as your body needs rest to recover after an intense workout, your brain also needs breaks. You can probably tell when

you have pushed yourself as far as you can mentally. You feel fried, you're not able to focus as well, and you see diminishing returns in terms of results. That's when a break will help you and your project.

- **Do all you can to get enough sleep.** You will function at a much higher level—thinking more clearly and creatively—when you get enough sleep. Plus, you will manage your stress better! A great book on the critical importance of sleep is *The Sleep Revolution* by Arianna Huffington (who collapsed from exhaustion and burnout, which spurred her to explore this topic).

Nurture a Positive Mindset: Get Rid of Negative Self-Beliefs

What we believe deeply matters. But if we believe something, does that necessarily make it true? (Let's remember our friends Santa, the Tooth Fairy, and the Easter Bunny…)

Fictional characters aside, what you believe about your public speaking skills definitely matters and can actually affect your performance. If you believe you're a terrible speaker and will probably mess up your talk, your performance might reflect those doubts and fears. On the other hand, if you believe you're the best person for the job and fully capable of nailing it (and you put time and effort in), your speech is likely to go much better.

Activity: Becoming Aware of Your Beliefs

You might never have stopped to consider what your beliefs in relation to public speaking are, so let's take an objective look at them now. Below is a list of statements. As you read each one, ask yourself if you think it is true or false.

I hate being the center of attention.	True	False
Everyone in the room is smarter than me.	True	False
I had a terrible and embarrassing experience while presenting in high school and I've never recovered! I know I'll never be good at it.	True	False
I am so nervous! This is awful. This means I will fail.	True	False
I am a boring speaker.	True	False
I know I'm going to screw this up!	True	False
I don't want anyone to see my hands shaking and my face turning bright red!	True	False
I have to get everyone in the room to like me.	True	False
I'm never going to be able to memorize all of my talk.	True	False
Everyone in the audience is going to be judging me, my appearance, and my performance.	True	False
I'm introverted, so I don't have what it takes to get up in front of people.	True	False
I just want to get this over with!	True	False
I will never have the confidence to do this well.	True	False
I am totally unqualified to do this.	True	False

If you answered "True" to many or most of these statements, you are carrying negative self-beliefs that are holding you back from giving your best performance.

How Do Negative Beliefs Affect Your Body?

Read through the list of statements in the "Becoming Aware of Your Beliefs" activity again and see how saying each belief makes your body feel. Do you feel panicked? Anxious? Angry? Are your palms sweaty? Is your heart racing? Are your cheeks flushed? Is your breath shallow? What a mess! Clearly, this is not how you want your body to feel right before you are going to present. While it's certainly okay to feel a bit nervous, you don't want to experience a full-body meltdown.

Sadly, many people buy into some or all of this type of negative self-talk, and therefore they avoid presenting whenever possible. They are missing out on exciting opportunities for growth, leadership, and making an impact because they believe these untruths about themselves.

How Do Positive Beliefs Affect Your Body?

If you find yourself engaging in or believing negative self-talk, it's not too late to change! But like anything else, it takes practice. Read through this list of positive beliefs.

- I got this!
- My unique perspective can make a difference.
- The message I am sharing is important.
- I am absolutely capable of learning new skills.
- I release the need to prove my worth.

- It's okay if I am nervous; accepting how I feel is better than fighting how I feel.
- I love sharing what I'm passionate about.
- I am enough.
- I'm excited to help people understand what I know.
- This experience is actually not about me. It's about affecting my audience in a positive way.
- Cool! This is a great opportunity to get out of my comfort zone and grow.

How did these statements make your body feel? Did you feel nervous but excited? Did you smile? Did you hold your head higher and stand up straighter? Notice how the positive words generated completely different physical reactions. That's why it's so important to become aware of negative self-talk, not buy into it, and focus on positive sentiments.

Activity: Change Negative Self-Talk Into Words of Encouragement

You can't expect to switch from tearing yourself down to building yourself up in one fell swoop. If reading some of the positive statements felt odd or embarrassing to you, rest assured that it's very normal. Here's how to practice feeling comfortable with them.

1. If you find it difficult to say the positive statements, you are hitting some resistance. Dig around to see what limited beliefs are making up that resistance. Chances are the limiting beliefs aren't true and can be changed.

2. Take some baby steps. You can potentially make a statement more palatable by adding some words to the belief:

- I am open to considering the idea that my unique perspective can make a difference.
- I am willing to entertain the notion that this experience is actually not about me.
- The message I am sharing might possibly be important.

3. Change a negative thought into a positive one (see the next section, "Cleaning Out Your Mental Closet," for more information).

The more you say these words aloud or to yourself, the more comfortable and nourished you'll feel. You'll also be changing your neural pathways in your brain for the better. (More on this topic here: https://anniewrightpsychotherapy.com/negative-thinking-which-wolf-feeding/.) Remember, timing is important. It's best not to pressure yourself to be more positive when you are cranky, overtired, or super hungry. In those moments take some deep breaths, eat some nourishing food, watch some comedy, connect with a friend who really gets you, or simply go to bed early.

Cleaning Out Your Mental Closet

Just like those old clothes that you need to donate to Goodwill, it's time to let go of the beliefs that no longer fit you, no longer serve you, and are no longer your style. Ditch those ideas (and garments) that make you feel inadequate and uncool. Your attachment to and identification with beliefs you've had for a long time can be like a sentimental feeling for a beat-up, pumpkin-colored sweater. You're so accustomed to these thoughts being a fixture in your inner landscape that you feel disoriented at the prospect of letting them go.

> **"No one can make you feel inferior without your consent."**
> **—Eleanor Roosevelt**

Even though it will feel different at first, wouldn't it feel better to only commit to beliefs that help you feel capable, inspired, and strong? Let those negative thoughts and feelings go. Clean out those closets, bureaus, basements, and attics of your mental and emotional archives.

Thought Bubbles

When a negative thought passes through your mind, take a deep belly breath. Then picture the negative belief inside a bubble. As you exhale, imagine that you are blowing away that bubble. Not only will this give you some helpful detachment, but you'll also feel more grounded in your body.

Once you've identified the negative beliefs that make up the pattern, you can start to address and replace them. As they cross your mind, observe and refuse to buy into them any longer. Don't let them hook you and take you on an emotionally negative ride.

Smiling at them is a tool to gain some much-needed distance as you start the process. *Oh, hello, belief. It is so funny to me that you are visiting! How cute. I can see you clearly now and I know that you are full of nonsense. How funny that you thought I would buy into you.*

For any of the negative beliefs you've been holding on to, write a new belief that contradicts the old one.

Here are some examples:

Old belief: I am unqualified to make this speech.
New belief: My unique perspective matters and my insights can make a difference.

Old belief: Sigh…I know that I am a boring speaker.
New belief: With some time and effort, I know I can figure out what's compelling and important about my subject matter.

Old belief: I just want to get this over with!
New belief: I am excited to stay in each moment of the story I am telling, so that my audience can receive it and my content can sink in. Pacing myself with pauses will help me with that.

Sometimes you may feel really stuck. When your mind is cluttered with many heavy, limited beliefs, you may feel like a turtle flipped on its back. You're disoriented, frustrated, and exerting a tremendous amount of effort but getting absolutely nowhere. When mental and emotional patterns hook us, that is what it feels like. It's exhausting, painful, and unproductive. There is no peace and no progress.

Reinforcing New Habits

When you are creating new, positive thought patterns, it's wise to reinforce them regularly. One way to do this is to write each belief on a separate notecard. Read them when you wake up and right before you go to bed. You could also read one each time you get up to get a glass of water at work. Reading them and saying them out loud regularly will help you to make them your own.

To flip you back onto your feet and reorient you toward a much stronger sense of self, commit to awareness, observation, and patience. The next time you feel like you are upside down or spinning your wheels, take some really deep breaths and observe what is happening internally. Take note of the beliefs and feelings that are swirling around. Do all you can to refrain from judging anything you observe. (This is very important, for when we judge, we add yet another unhelpful belief system to the pattern.) There may be some emotions associated with these old, unhelpful beliefs. As you sit with them, you may feel sad, angry, hurt, anxious, or other feelings. It's all okay. The best strategy here is to observe those emotions. Yes, you may feel vulnerable, but through this process you gain greater strength. Again, judgment will not serve you in any way.

Here's an example of an unhelpful negative judgment: *It is so stupid that I think this way! What is wrong with me? Why does this always happen? I'm never going to be free of these beliefs!*

Here's what observation and gentle acceptance sound like: *Okay. There is a lot going on here.* (Deep breath.) *This doesn't feel good at all. It's hard to take in what I am observing. I am increasingly aware that I have pain and anger connected to these beliefs.* (Deep breath.) *I don't like these beliefs that I am observing. They are really sad and mean.* (Deep breath.) *But the more awareness I have, the closer I am to letting go of what no longer serves me. This pattern is not me. This pattern is simply that, a pattern. And patterns can dissolve over time. That's enough for today! I need to go watch a comedy and have a nourishing snack. Tomorrow I'm going to do something really nice for myself!*

Remind yourself that you are simply watching and observing a pattern. Where do these patterns come from? Lots of places—possibly your family, your culture, your workplace, your experiences at school, your friends, and/or your spiritual or religious beliefs. This particular pattern may have scary and painful twists and turns, but it will even out and become calmer. Heighten your awareness so you can see what beliefs are at its core.

> *"It is the mark of an educated mind to be able to entertain a thought without accepting it."*
> —**Aristotle**

With each moment of increased awareness, you are starting to detach and dismantle the pattern, as though you were pulling a piece of yarn out of that orange sweater. It may take some time, but it is totally worth the effort! This is not necessarily a fun process, but when you bravely face your negative self-beliefs and dissolve them, it is amazing how much lighter you feel and how much more access to peace you have. When you have the courage to see things clearly, you gain a tremendous opportunity to build your independence, strength, and resilience. It can be helpful to share this process with a trusted and safe friend, family member, coach, and/or therapist. Support is a beautiful thing!

Avoid "Always" and "Never" Statements

Using the words *always* and *never* is not only inaccurate most of the time, but it is also a way to shut down your potential growth.

- I always get nervous.
- I'm never going to be good at this.

Always and *never* point to rigid, limiting beliefs that are lurking beneath the surface. Please don't always say never! Also, never say always! (See what I did there?)

Here are more nourishing and empowering beliefs to replace the previous ones:

- I sometimes get nervous and that's okay.
- I may not be as good at public speaking as I want to be right now, but I am committed to learning, growing, and improving.

Watch your language as you observe your self-talk and try to focus on realistic, positive statements.

Rewriting Your Worst-Case Scenario Public Speaking Stories

We often ascribe arbitrary meanings to our experiences. We create narratives about ourselves, events, and relationships to explain or justify situations that seem random, unstable, or even scary. If you are a fiction writer, this is a great skill! But the rest of us need to be aware of the stories we are creating and telling ourselves.

If you are expecting a friend to call you at eight p.m. and you still haven't heard from them by nine thirty p.m., it can be tempting to create a worst-case scenario story to explain what's happened. (They've been hit by a car! They don't want to be friends with me!)

You can see how these stories would lead to a hairy roller coaster ride of terror and grief. But when your friend finally calls at nine forty-five p.m., you find out their phone battery died, they had to work late, or they lost track of time. In the meantime you've been running down your own emotional battery with worry for nothing! It's very freeing to become aware when we are making up a story, whether it's about a delayed phone call or a public speaking experience.

> *"There is a vitality, a life force, an energy, a quickening that is translated through you into action, and because there is only one of you in all time, this expression is unique. And if you block it, it will never exist through any other medium and it will be lost."*
> —Martha Graham

To find your worst-case scenario storylines, be on the lookout for the phrase *that must mean*, as in, *That audience member seemed distracted. That must mean she hated my talk.*

Must it? It's possible that she may not have loved your talk. But what if she was inattentive because she just received a text from her manager alerting her that her company is holding an emergency board meeting? Or what if she had just gotten off the phone with her spouse, who told her that their son broke his leg on the playground?

Every audience member has a life with challenges, and sometimes their tough times are distracting. It's crucial that you stay the course with your focus, presence, and enthusiasm even if a few folks are not one hundred percent with you. If you continue to be compelling instead of getting wobbly, you may just draw their focus back to your message, even if they are going through something difficult.

Here's an old belief based on an arbitrary narrative, followed by a new belief based on a reality check:

Old belief: That audience member seemed distracted. That must mean she hated my talk.

New belief: That audience member seemed distracted. I don't know why. I'm going to dig deep into my own passion for this subject and not allow myself to be distracted from my mission.

Now that you are aware, you will probably notice when you create a narrative to justify an experience when you can't possibly have all of the facts. When this happens, examine the story closely to see if you can actually rely on it to be the truth. If you can't, let the arbitrary narrative go. Reframe your thoughts. It's okay to conclude that you just don't know.

The Trick to Dealing with the "Center of Attention" Conundrum

Picture yourself looking out at your audience. Who knows what kind of day all those people are having? Maybe the world news they read is making them depressed. Maybe one of them just got engaged. Maybe someone's kid has gotten in trouble at school. Maybe another one just got a big promotion.

Okay, folks are starting to put away their cell phones and look at you. In this moment you can either make *yourself* the center of your attention or make *your audience* the center of your attention.

When you make yourself the center of your attention, you may have thoughts along these lines:

- What are those audience members thinking about me?
- Why did I wear this outfit?
- Some people already look bored! Or mad!
- I bet they can tell I am nervous.

- OMG, I am sweating and shaking!
- I bet I seem fake.
- My voice sounds so weird!
- I'm just going to get this over with as fast as I can and put us all out of our misery.
- There are so many people looking at me! I know they are judging me!
- This is why I hate being the center of attention!

When you make *your audience* the center of your attention, you may have thoughts like these:

- I want these people to have a great experience that encourages them to see things differently.
- My message is more important than me looking absolutely perfect every moment. Passion is much more dynamic and memorable!
- I will look my audience in the eyes, to welcome them, see if they are following my story, and let them know I care.
- I am the host of this experience, which is exciting and could be fun.
- I am taking my audience on a fascinating tour of a world that I know. I want to show them the incredible things I've learned.
- A bigger crowd than I expected. Cool! There are now more people I can affect.
- So what if my hand is shaking a little or my cheeks are a bit red? I'm passionate about my important and urgent message.
- I want them to be able to see and hear me.

Making yourself the center of your own attention leads to self-consciousness and is absolutely no fun. When I discuss this concept during workshops, I use the following example. "Say you are sharing information about how the audience can help children get out of bleak poverty. You notice that you are becoming a little sweaty. What matters more: these vulnerable and suffering kids getting the help they need, or you looking calm and perfect? Wouldn't it be okay to get passionate about children who urgently need food, shelter, and education?"

Another way to think about this is: it's not about you.

Yes, you are the messenger. But this experience is really about an important message that needs to affect an audience so they can be transformed in some way. You can choose to make it all about you, but if you do that, everyone loses. The audience receives a fearful and self-conscious version of you, which then muddles your powerful message.

Choose win-win-win. Instead of viewing your audience as a firing squad, see them as guests whom you are excited to host. You can help these individuals see the world differently, see themselves differently, and become more empowered to take action. By simply shifting your perspective and making your audience the center of your attention, you can eliminate the whole "I hate being the center of attention" dilemma.

Caring...but Not Too Much

Remember Goldilocks? She is that girl who wandered into a bear family's home and tested out their food and furniture. Breaking and entering aside, Goldilocks has a lot to teach us about tenacity and self-care. Unsatisfied with mediocrity in her life, she tested bears' breakfasts, chairs, and beds to find the yummiest, most comfortable, "just right" fit for her needs.

What does this tale have to do with you and public speaking? Like Goldilocks, you can be choosy about the kinds of support and nourishment you give to yourself as you prepare to present. Goldilocks would try something, see how it felt, and when it felt "too hot," "too cold," "too hard," or "too soft," she moved on. She was on the lookout for what felt "just right."

Helping clients discern when their approach to a presentation, interview, or meeting is "too hard" or "too soft" is an important part of my coaching. Sometimes their attachment to a particular outcome is "too much." They care so much—*too* much—about what the audience may think, and/or they put a tremendous amount of pressure on themselves to be perfect. The resulting stress makes it difficult for them to creatively problem solve and present well.

On the other hand, sometimes clients care "too little." They don't put enough time into creating or rehearsing their presentation. They have yet to accept that excellence requires a lot of effort and commitment. Procrastination and fear of failure or success can also make it seem like a client cares "too little."

Caring too little or too much can sabotage your efforts. When Goldilocks realized that breakfast or furniture was "too this" or "too that," she kept moving forward, looking for better options. I encourage you to do the same. If you care too much, you may be incredibly stressed and driven by joyless perfectionism. If you care too little, you may feel unmotivated and avoidant. Whatever the case, it's time to assess and adjust your beliefs so that your amount of caring truly serves you and feels "just right." This balance will help you feel nourished, motivated, and supported in your work.

When coaching, I navigate how to best support my client during each session. There are moments when I sense that it's best to be gentle and times when being direct and tough is the right approach. Sometimes humor and playfulness are a great plan, while in other moments seriousness is the optimal choice for growth. When I see the proverbial light bulb go on—something has clicked or my client had an epiphany—I know a "just right" moment has happened. The client is relieved, breathes easier, and says things like: "Oh, I get it!" "Oh, that makes so much sense!" "That makes me feel much better." You should look for these same moments as you think about your approach to public speaking.

Caring Too Little

Here's a story about a client of mine who started out caring "too little." Liam came to work with me after going on a round of unsuccessful interviews at a number of institutions. He was disappointed about the missed opportunities and wanted to improve his chances for future interactions with potential employers.

Before his first round of interviews, Liam didn't want to put too much pressure on himself. In hopes of avoiding being really stressed, he told himself, "It's not that big a deal." As a result he started to care "too little." He didn't put a lot of time into his preparation, and he neglected to develop presentation skills for these valuable opportunities.

There was another problem too. Liam had a PhD in the field of social work. For years he had been examining aspects of a broken system in great depth, and over time he had lost faith that the system would ever get better. Not only did Liam enter each interview telling himself, "This is not a big deal," but he also came in the room weary about his subject. In this instance his despair about the system meant he cared too much and was carrying too much baggage.

After presenting his job talk at various institutions, the feedback was consistent. It seemed to his audience (the people who were hiring) that he didn't want to be there. Liam was told that he seemed weary and a bit frustrated when audience members asked him questions about his research. This response was interpreted as annoyance, which in reality was his loss of faith manifesting.

These were not good impressions and were costing him greatly. When we started working together, we discussed the feedback and what he could do to shift the impression he was making. It was understandable and wise that Liam did not want to increase his anxiety by fixating on "the incredible importance of these interviews." In Liam's circumstances it could be tempting to think, *This institution is so impressive! I have to be perfect!* But he didn't want to fall into the trap of caring too much either.

How could he align himself with helpful attitudes that honored his recognition that these were amazing opportunities and that he did care about his performance? Could Liam shift his emotional heaviness about his subject matter so that his palpable weariness didn't put off his listeners during the Q&A? Let's get some help for Liam from our friend Goldilocks. As we know, she is good at determining what really works.

WWGS

What would Goldilocks say? Let's have her test these belief systems.

Liam: "This institution is so impressive! I have to be perfect!"
Goldilocks: "These beliefs are too stressful."

Liam: "It's not that big a deal."
Goldilocks: "This belief is too lax. You won't be motivated to do your best."

Liam: "This is a really cool opportunity. I'm excited to share what I've learned with my audience. I do have some heaviness and despair about my topic. I need to take a step back to rediscover what I initially found fascinating and important about this subject and share from that

perspective. If I really think about it, perhaps I may inspire someone in my audience to dig deep and figure out how to fix this broken system!"
Goldilocks: "These beliefs are 'just right'—inspiring and empowering."

Caring Too Much

Caring about your audience, your subject matter, your delivery, and the outcome is important. However, if you care too much about what your audience thinks of you, you can sabotage your best efforts.

Consider Mariana. She had been recently hired to be the VP of marketing at a *Fortune* 500 company. Mariana is Brazilian-born and English is her second language. Her department was predominantly male and Caucasian. When we first met, Mariana said she was distracted by caring too much about how her colleagues might be viewing her. She was concerned that they thought she didn't belong because she was different. These concerns were getting in the way of her concentration and confidence. Her thoughts were becoming increasingly negative and anxious.

It is essential to consider your audience, but in this case Mariana's concerns about her audience were painfully getting in her way. Yes, as a woman of color in the room, she was outnumbered by Caucasian men. Yes, she was from a country outside of the US, English was her second language, and there were many Americans in the room. These were facts and Mariana had a choice as to how she framed these facts. I didn't want her to be overwhelmed and disempowered by the way she thought.

WWGS

What would Goldilocks say? Let's have Goldilocks test Mariana's belief systems.

Mariana: "They are not going to take me seriously because I am different in so many ways."
Goldilocks: "This belief is way too stressful."

Mariana: "I don't look like I belong here."
Goldilocks: "No. This belief is too limited."

Mariana: "This is a really great opportunity. Yes, I am different from the rest of the people in the room. This is actually my strength. I am excited to share my unique perspective with my audience. My point of view is valuable. This group and its goals will only benefit from diverse opinions. I am excited to contribute. Also, my presence will challenge the status quo and will model diversity to others who feel different."
Goldilocks: "Yes! These beliefs feel 'just right.'"

Real-World Example:
How Caring "Just Right" Helped a Team

Years ago I performed in an original play that received rave reviews. When reviewers from a local TV show came to see the production, they loved the show so much that they sent a few folks from their team to tape a very small segment of the show. They did this during the day, with cast members who were available at the time.

The night the episode aired, the host of the TV show sat with the reviewers. At the beginning of the segment, the short clip of the play they had recorded aired. The host was not impressed. Mind you, he had not been to see the show; he just saw a very short, out-of-context clip. His comment? "This looks terrible." The reviewers who had seen the entire live performance immediately jumped in to defend the show.

The next day, as I approached the theater, I felt awkward about the comments about the play I had heard on TV the night before. I wasn't sure if other cast members had watched the TV show, so I decided not to bring it up. I didn't want to disturb anyone's concentration.

When I entered the theater, what I saw blew me away and made me laugh. Our director, an extremely funny guy, had created many small posters that included a picture of the host and his blunt comments about the show. He had hung them in the lobby and all over the dressing rooms.

This was not to punish or haunt the cast. His intention was to face the nonsense and laugh at it. He didn't want us to avoid it—he wanted the cast and crew to look it in the eye and then move past it.

It worked. The tense situation was diffused in a "just right" way, and the host's ill-informed words had no power over us at all.

CHAPTER 3

Empowering Yourself Physically

The way you stand, the way you sit, the way you hold yourself, and the way you cross the stage all influence the people watching and listening to you. But did you know that these things also affect you and your confidence? In this chapter you'll learn how to make empowered physical choices that will not only increase your stage presence but will also help you feel more courageous. I'll cover the age-old question "What do I do with my hands?" as well as what to do with your feet when you're standing still and moving across the stage.

The Impact of Your Body Language

How you feel inside and the way you position your body are inextricably connected. Think of actors—they use physical choices like posture and other mannerisms to help create characters. Not only do these choices create a visual picture for the audience, but their body language also alters the actors' internal landscape, emotionally and intellectually, to help actors feel like they are inhabiting those characters.

Even if you are not a professional actor, you already play a number of roles in your day-to-day life. You may be a boss, a mother, a daughter, and a client. You may be a husband, a teacher, a student, and a volunteer. You're still you, but you draw upon different skill sets, knowledge, and/or communication styles depending upon which role you are playing at any given moment. And your body language will often change to match your role.

As you heighten your awareness around your physical language as it relates to public speaking, you'll discover which choices really serve and empower you and which are disempowering.

A wonderful artist, teacher, and friend of mine, Eliza Ryan, shared the following exercises with me. She has helped countless actors create compelling characters using these tools and now uses them to teach organizations how to build creativity and develop empathy. Once I witnessed how powerful, and in some ways simple, these exercises are for actors, I understood how they could also be of great help to people wanting to build their confidence and speak publicly.

Activity: Exploring Body Language Choices

This activity will ask you to adopt various body positions and see what your resulting feelings are. It will be easier to explore these steps if you are by yourself at home, or with a friend who also wants to try this out. Find a room where you can walk around and not trip over furniture, electrical cords, etc. If you feel self-conscious at first, no worries. Just keep trying different choices. As you do, observe how each choice makes you feel and see what thoughts come forward. If you have a hard time committing fully to the first few choices, when you complete all of them, come back to the early ones and try them again.

As you follow the directions and explore the different physical choices, ask yourself, does the body language choice:

- Increase or decrease your confidence?
- Make it easier or more difficult to breathe?
- Bring your attention to your inner world or the outer world around you?
- Lead you to feeling sad, aggressive, happy, flirty, peaceful, or otherwise?

The following are seventeen different physical choices for you to explore:

1. **DIRECT:** Stand up straight, with your feet about hip-distance apart. Place your arms by your sides. Face forward. Now walk around the room in a direct manner.
2. **INDIRECT:** Stand with your body facing slightly left or right, head down, with your feet about hip-distance apart. Your arms may be in front of you or your hands may be in your pockets. This

posture should not look anything like the DIRECT one you just did. Now walk around the room in an indirect manner.

3. **OPEN:** Stand up straight with your feet about hip-distance apart. Roll back your shoulders and open your arms and chest. Hold your arms by your sides. Imagine that your heart and mind are wide open. Now walk around the room in this open manner.

4. **CLOSED:** Stand up straight with your feet about hip-distance apart. Cross your arms in front of you. Imagine that your mind and heart are closed. Now walk around the room in this closed manner.

5. **BUBBLY:** Stand up straight with your feet about hip-distance apart. Place your arms loosely by your sides. Put some spring in your step, like you are full of seltzer. Now walk around the room and be bubbly.

6. **TIGHT:** Stand up straight with your feet close together. Place your arms by your sides. Tighten as many muscles as you can. Face forward. Now walk around the room in a tight manner. You can also explore what happens when you quicken your pace a bit.

7. **LOOSE:** Shake out your arms and legs to fully let go of TIGHT. Keep your body loose as you explore the room. Let your face, neck, back, and leg muscles relax as much as possible.

8. **HEAVY:** Stand still with your feet about hip-distance apart. Place your arms by your sides. Imagine that your body feels very heavy, as if you are weighted down. Now walk around the room with this sense of heaviness.

9. **LIGHT:** Let go of the heaviness. Stand up straight with your feet about hip-distance apart. Place your arms by your sides. Allow your body to feel very light, as if you're a balloon filled with helium. Walk around the room with this sense of lightness.

10. **BRIGHT:** Shift from LIGHT to BRIGHT. Stand up straight with your feet about hip-distance apart. Place your arms by your sides.

11. **HARD:** Stand up straight with your feet about hip-distance apart. Your arms can be crossed or by your sides. Imagine that your body has a hard shell and your heart has hardened too. Face forward. Now walk around the room.

12. **SOFT:** Let the hard shell you created completely dissolve. Stand up straight with your feet about hip-distance apart. Place your arms by your sides and allow your heart to soften. Now walk around the room and explore this sense of softness.

13. **SPARKLY:** Stand up straight with your feet about hip-distance apart. SPARKLE it up! See what this direction means to you as you walk around the room in a sparkly manner—you may be smiling, flirty, or energetic.

14. **SHALLOW:** Stand up straight with your feet about hip-distance apart. Place your arms by your sides. Face forward. Now explore the room from a shallow perspective. When I am in this mode, I find that I do not have a long attention span. I observe things around me briefly and feel a bit judgmental.

15. **DEEP:** Let go of SHALLOW. Stand up straight with your feet about hip-distance apart. Place your arms by your sides. Explore what it means to physically embody depth. You may not feel a need to move much at all. As you do this, contemplate the impact you want to make on the world with your work.

16. **SMALL:** Stand still with your feet close together. Place your arms by your sides. Take up as little space as possible. Now walk around the room, again making your body occupy as little space as possible.

17. **BIG:** Stand up straight with your feet about hip-distance apart. Place your arms by your sides. Don't be afraid to let your body take up space. Face forward. Now walk around the room with this sense of BIG. (This does not mean arrogant. If you start thinking, *I am big, I am bigger and better than everyone else*, then take it down a notch or two. Simply be. It may be helpful to add an element of SOFT or OPEN. Take up space and let go of any kind of comparison.)

A note about SMALL and BIG—even if you are petite in stature, you can still be BIG! Think about Malala Yousafzai. She is a Pakistani activist for female education and the youngest ever Nobel Prize laureate. Malala is 5'3", but she has a huge presence and has already made a powerful impact on the world. Also, even if you are really large in stature, you can still be SMALL. In the movie *The Blind Side* the character Michael Oher (played by Quinton Aaron, who is 6'8") is very tall, but in the early stages of the movie, when he is overwhelmed and lost, his presence is smaller thanks to his defeated looks and such.

Once you've finished each option, reflect on your experiences.

- Which choices felt empowering?
- Which choices felt disempowering?
- Were there choices that felt familiar? If so, which ones? For some people CLOSED or INDIRECT is a default. On some level it feels safer. If this is true for you, take note of any other feelings or thoughts that come to mind when you choose CLOSED or INDIRECT.
- Which choices allowed you to breathe the most easily?
- Did you find that your relationship with yourself was affected by your physical choices?

Layering Your Choices

Now let's try to use two different physical choices simultaneously. Walk around the room and combine:

- BIG and DIRECT
- SMALL and INDIRECT
- OPEN and BUBBLY
- HEAVY and CLOSED
- LOOSE and OPEN
- TIGHT and FAST
- SMALL and SOFT
- LOOSE and DEEP
- BIG and SPARKLY

Once you've finished each combination, reflect on your experiences.

- Which combination is the most empowering for you?
- Which is the least?
- Which put you in the most creative mood?
- Which put you in the most upbeat mood?
- Which was the biggest downer?

Certain specific physical choices can help you to think more creatively as you prepare to speak in public. Now you have a range of options available to you. When you determine which ones are most empowering for you, see if you can find music that you like that encourages you to make those physical choices.

Which Body Language Options Are the Best for Public Speaking?

In general I have found BIG, OPEN, and DIRECT—with some BRIGHT or SPARKLY—to be helpful for me and many of my clients. That said, it's important to understand who your audience is and identify your objective or goal for your talk. That will always help you determine the most effective choices for your situation.

> ## When Choosing HEAVY Is Helpful
>
> When I am leading body language choice exercises, HEAVY is not my favorite. I tend to feel sad and less hopeful when I explore it. But if I have too many things on my mind and feel like my thoughts are spinning, I can find it helpful to feel a bit of HEAVY in my feet and legs. It grounds me in my body and helps me clear my head.

The following are several public speaking scenarios, the speaker's goals for each, and body language choices that support those goals.

Scenario: A new volunteer needs to introduce himself to a group of teens at an after-school program.
Goals: To be friendly, fun, and confident
Body Language Choices: BIG, OPEN, DIRECT, and BUBBLY

Scenario: An activist is speaking to a crowd about recent losses in their community.
Goals: To empathize, acknowledge the loss and grief, and offer words of comfort
Body Language Choices: BIG, OPEN, and SOFT

Scenario: A maid of honor is toasting her best friend at her wedding.
Goals: To let the audience know about fun times they've shared, pranks they've played, how the bride is a great friend, how smitten the bride is with her groom, and that they are a great match for one another
Body Language Choices: BIG, OPEN, SOFT, and SPARKLY; BIG, OPEN, and DIRECT; or BIG, OPEN, and DEEP (depending on the personality of the maid of honor)

Scenario: A manager has to gather her team to let them know that if the company doesn't hit certain sales targets, there may be layoffs.
Goals: To convey the stakes of the situation in a direct, confident, and clear manner
Body Language Choices: What would you choose?

You don't always need to use all of your choices simultaneously. You may want to start with one type of energy and shift to another.

Sometimes Getting Small Can Serve You

In general people do not like the physical choice of SMALL. When they take up less space, they often feel insecure, invisible, and vulnerable. One day I was leading a workshop for pediatricians and they shared that getting physically smaller was a good idea when they were speaking to children. They didn't want to intimidate young kids by towering over them, which was wise. That's why it's always important to remember what choices will serve your audience and let that information guide you.

Real-World Example:
Carlos Experiences the Impact of Body Language on His
Audience, Even When They Can't See Him!

You've been learning that your physical choices affect both you and your audience. What's really interesting is that your body language can actually influence your audience even when they can't see you. Here's an example that illustrates this compelling point.

My new client, Carlos, enjoys the fact that he works from home for part of his week. Much of his job consists of cold-calling prospects, which could be nerve-racking. Making a good impression very quickly is critical to his success. During our first session he realized how his choice of body language made a big impact on his confidence and also on his ability to communicate clearly and powerfully: "I think part of my problem, or maybe the biggest part of my problem, is that I am always making my calls sitting down, hunched over my phone. When I'm at work, I'm trying not to disturb anyone, and when I'm at home, I'm in casual mode, wearing really casual clothes. I don't think my clothing is helping me feel my best." I added that being hunched over makes it difficult to breathe deeply, which can also undermine confidence.

We then prepared to role-play a cold call. First, he embodied BIG, OPEN, and DIRECT. He walked around the room to inhabit this new mode. We then stood in different parts of the room, not looking at each other, so that the situation was truer to a phone call, where you don't have the benefit of any visual cues. Then he "called" me and gave me his pitch.

When he was BIG, OPEN, and DIRECT, Carlos was self-assured, and any tentativeness or self-consciousness he had displayed earlier was gone. He wasn't too pushy or aggressive; instead, he came across as a good listener who was capable, caring, and knowledgeable. Carlos guided the conversation but was flexible enough to go with the flow when I asked questions. Acting BIG gave Carlos a sense of empowerment and cleared his mind. Embodying DIRECT helped him to guide the conversation and get to the point quickly. The OPEN approach enabled him to be an adaptive, thoughtful listener who didn't need to control every moment of the call to make things happen.

At the end of our session Carlos declared that he would try to make all of his calls from home, where he felt comfortable taking up space. We agreed that a headset could really be an asset for him. He also decided that he would dress professionally at home so that he felt more polished and confident.

Activity: Does Body Language Affect Your Verbal Language?

We have explored how body language bears a direct relation to how you feel, so it's logical that it may also affect what you say and how you say it. Stand up and think about your favorite TV show or movie. Now talk about it for a couple of minutes using each of these combinations:

- BIG and DIRECT
- SMALL and INDIRECT
- OPEN and BUBBLY
- HEAVY and CLOSED
- LOOSE and OPEN
- TIGHT and FAST
- SMALL and SOFT
- LOOSE and DEEP
- BIG and SPARKLY

When you're done with the list, reflect on how each combination affected what you said and how you said it.

1. What types of differences did you notice?
2. Which options gave you the biggest contrast?
3. Which options felt the best?

Focus On What You Want to Be, Not What You Don't Want to Be

Clients often begin by telling me what they *don't* want to be when they imagine giving a speech or leading a meeting:

- "I don't want to come across as too aggressive."
- "I don't want to come across as too angry."
- "I don't want to come across as too big in this small conference room."
- "I don't want to come across as too small on that huge stage."
- "I don't want to seem like I don't know what I'm talking about."
- "I don't want to seem like I'm trying too hard."

When I say any of these statements to myself, I can feel my body contract in fear. And it feels bad. It is much more straightforward and expansive when we focus on what we *want* to do and be rather than what we don't. Instead of thinking about what you are trying to avoid, consider the approaches in the "Exploring Body Language Choices" activity in this chapter and choose the options that match your goals as a speaker.

Expanding versus Contracting

When life offers us big circumstances (be they huge opportunities or immense challenges), we can physically contract or expand. When situations feel too big (you've lost your job, you've landed your dream job and now have a lot of new responsibilities, you are dealing with difficult people at work or home), choose expansion—choose BIG and OPEN. When you expand your physicality, your thinking will be clearer and your confidence will increase.

Activity: Exploring Sitting

Most of us sit down without thinking much about it. Let's bring some awareness to sitting by following these steps:

1. Sit in a chair. Take up as little space as possible. Note how this choice affects your level of confidence. Notice how easy or difficult it is to breathe.
2. Shift the way you are sitting so that you are now taking up as much space as possible. Note how this new choice affects your level of confidence. Notice how easy or difficult it is to breathe.
3. Shift the way you are sitting so that you are taking up the space you need while sitting appropriately for work. Are you BIG, OPEN, DIRECT, and LOOSE? Is it easy to breathe? If the answers are yes, then not only will this choice help you to feel more confident, but you'll also project a more confident presence.

How to Present When You're Sitting Down

Thus far in this chapter we've explored body language choices that help you feel empowered while standing and walking. Now we'll focus on confidently giving a talk while sitting, which might happen when you're in smaller settings.

During my workshops I address questions about sitting by asking the whole class to sit "small, closed, and tight." Next, I tell the class to sit "big, open, and loose." We then discuss what feels and looks the best for everyone. We typically find that having your arms open looks and feels more powerful. Your arms can rest on the arms of the chair, by your sides, or on the table. Many people are not fans of "manspreading" (when guys on otherwise open public transportation benches sit with their legs wide apart and take up more space than they really need), so it's wise to stay away from this behavior in all arenas. Crossing your legs might feel more comfortable depending on what you are wearing.

Real-World Example:
Sophia Gets More Comfortable with Standing While Presenting

If offered a choice of sitting or standing while giving a talk, most people would happily sit. Sitting makes many speakers feel less exposed, less nervous, and less distracted. This was especially true of my client Sophia. During a recent session she expressed that when she stands to present, she immediately feels tight and anxious, and the room suddenly feels formal and less intimate. A few days earlier she had spoken to an audience while seated. She experienced no self-consciousness, felt like herself, and authentically shared about a subject she cares about—alleviating postpartum depression.

Clearly, Sophia was very sold on the advantages of sitting. To challenge her thinking, I asked her to tell me why standing could potentially be the best choice for her upcoming talk. She thought for a moment and listed the following:

- My audience will see me better, which is good because my topic is really important.
- I will feel freer to use my body and hands to express myself.
- My audience will probably respect me more if I'm standing up in front of them.

I added that people tend to have a lot more energy when they stand. With that, I could see her resistance start to shift.

Sophia practiced her talk on her feet. When she felt too formal or stiff, I encouraged her to shake out her arms and remember how she felt emotionally when sitting. I reminded her that, with the right mindset, she could have the same sense of intimacy and connection with her audience as she did when sitting. By her last run-through Sophia said she really did think standing was the best choice in terms of feeling empowered and getting her important message out to everyone in the room.

If you have dreaded standing, like Sophia did, challenge yourself to explore what advantages it brings you and your speech. Then focus on mirroring the ease and confidence you enjoy in a sitting position in a standing one.

What Do I Do with My Hands?

"What do I do with my hands?!" is in the top three questions I am asked as a public speaking consultant. I think that people would love to have more than two hands to get things done in their daily lives. They'd be psyched to have extra help juggling their tech gadgets, coffee, gym clothes, and groceries. But then, when they're onstage, they rue the day they were cursed...with hands!

When Your Hands Are Moving

There's not only one proper way to use your hands when presenting. Certain hand gestures can be distracting and unhelpful, however. The bottom line is that people have their own personal rhythm. In terms of specific gestures, most can work well if they help you tell your story. Usually your hands will organically find their way in terms of movement while you are speaking.

During workshops, I will ask for a volunteer to tell a story about something they love in front of the group. What typically happens is that without much effort at all the hands communicate clearly—they help to emphasize certain points, demonstrate the shapes and sizes of what the speaker is describing, express emotion, and can sometimes even add humor!

When you are able to fully inhabit your body, rather than being in your head or self-conscious, that natural rhythm is more likely to come through and your hand gestures will go with your flow and make sense. A recent workshop attendee put it perfectly when he told a fellow student, "When you were one with your story, your body language and gestures came together seamlessly." Remember, your message is more important than you. Let your hand gestures serve your message.

That said, stay away from any racy or rude gestures. A trusted friend or, colleague, or a video of a rehearsal can help you to discover which choices are working and if anything is awkward or distracting. For example, you might frequently touch your hair or glasses, or scratch your face without even realizing it. It will also help you to see if you need to make any adjustments in regards to how you are holding your notes, a microphone, a laser pointer, or the clicker for your slides. You'll learn some tips for holding these types of items near the end of Chapter 4.

When Your Hands Are Still

Let's review some options for what to do with your hands and arms when they are not moving.

- Arms hanging naturally by your sides. I am not suggesting that you stay like this for your entire talk; that would be strange. But this is a nice open position to be in briefly from time to time.
- One hand holding the other in front of you, with your arms relaxed. If your arms are tight and it looks like you are holding on to yourself for dear life, then this will not work so well.
- Arms hanging in front of you, with palms facing each other and the tips of your fingers touching.

I'm not a fan of these choices:

- Hands in pockets
- Hands behind your back
- Arms crossed in front of your chest
- Using only one hand to gesture, while the other one hangs idly

That said, if you are doing any of these to illustrate a point or for comedic effect, then by all means go for it.

What Do I Do with My Feet?

Your body is a physical vehicle for your ideas. You will want your physical choices to serve your message, rather than distract from it.

I typically get fewer questions from clients about what to do with their feet than I do about their hands. But what you choose to do with your feet and movement matters just as much. If you want your audience to buy into your message, contribute to your cause, or follow your example, they need to trust you. They need to see a solid and grounded individual who is open, confident, and worthy of attention and respect.

Stillness Is Powerful

Purposeful stillness is different than being frozen like a deer in headlights. When you are alert and still, your feet solidly on the ground, hip-distance apart, you will draw the audience's eyes to you. You certainly do not need to be still for your entire talk. But when you are making key points, be still. You do not want random movements to undermine the power of your message.

Standing with your feet hip-distance apart is a much more powerful and grounded stance than when your feet are right next to each other. The first option is expansive and helps you to look more like a leader; the second one makes you seem smaller. You don't need to stand with your legs wide apart like you are a cowboy in a Wild West saloon duel. Just place your feet on the floor, right beneath your hips.

Don't favor one foot over the other, meaning don't lean on one while bending your other knee. This looks too casual. Also, don't lock your knees; this is not a stable position. Keep your knees slightly bent. That said, if any of these positions help you to make a point or add a comedic moment, include them!

Shifting, Rocking, and Randomly Moving Are Distracting

Beware of shifting your weight around too much. When people are uncomfortable being onstage, they can end up moving unnecessarily while standing. Some people shift their weight from one foot to the other, rocking from side to side. Others place one foot ahead, one foot behind, and rock forward and back. Not only are these choices distracting for your audience, but they are also distracting for you.

There are some speakers who try to manage their nervous energy by randomly moving around. I find this to be really distracting. It does not help the audience focus on the ideas and information being shared. I remember one client whose physicality and movement were initially serving him and his message during his rehearsal with me. But when he started talking about the money he needed to raise for his venture, he took a step backward. It made him look tentative and sheepish. This action did not inspire confidence. In fact, it led me to question his message.

How to Move with a Purpose

Just as you want every word you share to be motivated by a reason, you also want your movement to have a positive purpose. It's important to time your movement well. You want the timing to support your talk, rather than distract from it.

Here is a very simple guideline: if you are saying something really important, be still. If you are making a content transition, feel free to take a few steps to a different part of the stage. Here's an example:

(Enjoy stillness as you say these statements that provide vital context.)

"What do the Amur leopard, the black rhino, the Bornean orangutan, and the eastern lowland gorilla have in common? These and fourteen other species are on the World Wildlife Fund critically endangered list. The World Wildlife Fund is the world's leading conservation organization and makes an impact in one hundred countries."

(Transitional sentence—this is a fine time to move.)

"There are a number of ways that you can take action to help protect these vulnerable animals."

(This action step is important information, so be still.)

"First, you can get the word out about the urgent need for conservation through the World Wildlife Fund's Action Center."

(You could move on "The second thing you can do?" and then stay still for the details that follow.)

"The second thing you can do? Adopt an animal *(pause)* symbolically! When you purchase an adoption kit for a penguin, panda, polar bear, or other animal, not only will you receive a really cuddly plush toy. You'll also get an adoption certificate, a photo of your animal, and an animal data sheet."

(You could move on "The third action you can take" and then stay still for the rest of the sentence.)

"The third action you can take—you can contribute valuable financial support."

Walking and Talking in the Aisles

If you have a clear path, walking down the aisles to be closer to your audience can help the experience feel more intimate for them and for you. If you make this choice, just be careful that your volume still works for the room. If there are people behind you, speak louder, since you are no longer facing all of your audience.

The same "moving with a purpose" guidelines apply here. Be still when you are making key points. Intentionally move when you are saying transitional sentences.

Your Movement Can Help Deter Side Conversations

If a few people in my audience are chatting to each other while I am speaking, I will casually walk over and stand near them when possible. I don't glare at them; I don't kick their seats. I smile and continue speaking, which brings the attention of the room to where they are. This usually results in their conversation ending.

Your physical preparation will go a long way toward helping you feel less nervous, and will help you feel like your body language is working for you. My hope is that going forward you will be intentional about your physicality, so that you can make choices that lead you to feeling confident, grounded, and able to breathe easily.

CHAPTER 4

Empowering Yourself Vocally

You may have created the most profound, intelligent, and witty presentation that ever existed, but if you have not developed your vocal skills, your talk could fall flat and bore your audience. That's why it is critical to invest time into exploring a variety of creative ways to express the words you wrote.

In this chapter you'll learn how to have proper breath support so people can hear you, your voice can sound its best, and you can feel more grounded. I'll explain what vocal variety is, why it is important, and how you can incorporate it into your communication. You'll also learn to watch for habits such as vocal fry, upspeak, and filler words. Non-native English speakers sometimes have concerns about speaking with an accent, so I'll cover this topic as well. Lastly, I'll describe different types of microphones to amplify your voice and how best to use them.

Breathing

Most of the time you breathe without thinking about it. When you have to speak in public, however, you may suddenly notice that your breath becomes faster and shallower. In those moments it can also be hard to think clearly. The quality of your breathing affects:

- Your vocal expression (e.g., the quality of your voice, resonance)
- Your sense of calm, excitement, or panic
- Your ability to think clearly
- Your ability to feel grounded in your body

It's important to have breathing strategies so that you can consciously manage your breathing and allow it to support your voice, your mental processes, and your sense of well-being.

Beware of Long Sentences

Many people like to say one long run-on sentence or multiple sentences on one breath. By the time they finish speaking they feel panicked, their vocal quality has been compromised, and it is harder for their audience to understand them. It is a lose-lose-lose situation. When I notice a client doing this, I encourage them to speak in shorter sentences and/or to take more breaths. This will demand less from their breathing and also make it easier for them to be understood.

Belly Breathing

Belly breathing, also known as "diaphragmatic breathing," can help you manage your breath as you speak. (Your diaphragm is a dome-shaped muscle situated at the base of your lungs.) When you become aware that you are breathing more shallowly, you can make an adjustment and change course. If you are a singer or actor, if you play an instrument like a flute or trumpet, or if you do yoga, you probably already use diaphragmatic breathing or belly breathing. If none of those categories applies to you, here's your chance to see what all of the fuss is about.

Activity: Belly Breathing

This exercise will show you how to notice and direct your breath in certain ways. First, just practice observing your breath:

1. Lie on your back on the floor or on your bed or sofa. Let your whole body relax. You can prop up your knees and head if that is more comfortable.
2. Put one palm just below your ribs and place the other on your upper chest.
3. Now take a breath in through your nose and allow the breath to expand into your belly area, as though your belly were a balloon. Your hand will rise. Your other hand, which is resting on your upper chest, should not be moving much at all.

Internally, when you inhale your diaphragm contracts, leaving more space in your chest cavity for your lungs to expand and fill with air. Try the following steps five times:

1. Allow your body to be relaxed as you breathe in through your nose. Fill up your belly area and then breathe out. Repeat.
2. Now breathe in again and fill up. Let all of the air out until there is absolutely no air left. I don't want you to pass out, but go for as long as you can, and then take a deep breath in. You should feel your diaphragm working as it contracts and expands.
3. Try this three more times so you can really feel your diaphragm at work.
4. To make belly breathing a habit, do these exercises ten to twenty minutes daily.

Isn't it soothing? The next time you are stressed, see if this exercise can calm you down. Breathing in this way is your secret weapon for rich vocal quality, feeling more grounded, and increasing your presence.

Projection

Diaphragmatic breathing is directly linked to your ability to project your voice. (It will help if you complete the "Belly Breathing" activity before exploring this section.) If you have ever lost your voice because of yelling at a sporting event, loud party, or bar, you were probably projecting by pushing from your throat. This is not a healthy way to be heard, and as you've experienced, it is not physically sustainable. Your diaphragm is the muscle that will help you to project in a smart way.

The following "Learning How to Project" activity and the later section on "Volume" will help you practice this skill.

Activity: Learning How to Project

For the following activity you will breathe the way you learned to in the "Belly Breathing" activity.

1. Lie on your back on the floor or on your bed or sofa. Prop up your head and knees if that is more comfortable. Place one palm on the area just below your ribs and place the other on your upper chest. Let your whole body relax. Take a deep inhale (your lower hand will rise), and when you let it out, make a "sssss" sound. You will sound like a snake or leaky tire. Let out all of the air on this "sssss" sound until you have to take another breath. Try this three more times.

2. For the next set, make an "ooooo" sound (as in "food"). Allow your body to be relaxed and your throat to open. Take a deep inhale, and let it out on this sound. Try this three more times. At this point my hope is that you are feeling that flow and placement of breath as you inhale and exhale. You should be feeling how your breath is supporting the sound you are making.

3. It's time to experiment with volume. Allow your body to be relaxed and your throat to open. Take a deep inhale, and let it out on the "ooooo" sound. After three seconds, increase your volume for two counts. Then decrease your volume. Take a breath when you need one. Your diaphragm needs to be the muscle that is enabling you to modulate your volume. Do not push using your throat muscles. Try this three more times.

4. Now slowly stand up. Put your hands in the same position—one resting on your upper chest, the other placed just below your ribs. You're going to inhale in the same way, and then exhale on the "ooooo" sound. Take note if when you do this your shoulders go

up. There's no need for them to rise when you take a breath in. Let your belly area expand instead. Try this three more times. By doing this, you are allowing your lungs to fill with more oxygen, which your body loves!

5. Now breathe in again, and on the exhale say, "Hello." Again, your goal is to allow your breath to support the sound. Your breath is the wave, and your words are the surfer.

6. Gradually add more words, such as, "Hello. My name is _____ (your name here)." You may need to take a breath after "Hello." It's okay if your words feel really slow. Focus on properly supporting your words; you can speed up once you get the hang of it.

7. Now try to say a few sentences. You may need to take a few more breaths. Go slowly.

8. As you speak, increase your volume. Let your diaphragm be the muscle that enables you to be louder. This is how you project in a healthy way that is sustainable if you need to be loud for an extended period of time.

Vocal Variety

One of the biggest reasons audience members lose interest during a presentation is because the speaker is droning on and on with very little vocal variety. Their tone, volume, and inflection remain the same throughout.

When musicians read sheet music, they see musical notations indicating when it is time to get louder or softer, go faster or slower, play higher or lower notes, or be silent. The composer has written these directions into the score so that the music will create a specific experience for the audience. Whether the song is "Purple Rain," "Single Ladies," Mozart's Piano Concerto No. 21, or "The Star-Spangled Banner," the musicians know what to do.

Whether you're the creator of your own talk or champion of someone else's slides, you will not have these helpful notations to guide you. It is your job to artfully make these choices for yourself.

You have some very simple tools at your disposal to help you mix it up vocally. When speaking, you can vary your:

- Pitch
- Pace
- Pauses
- Volume
- Tone, which is determined by your intention (to be explored in Chapter 7)

Varying these elements in service of the story you are telling will make your words more enjoyable to listen to, exciting, and memorable.

Pitch

Pitch is the degree of highness or lowness of a tone. You are more likely to keep the audience engaged if you modulate your voice, using a range of pitches throughout your talk.

We have all had that teacher or professor who, though their subject matter was fascinating, had such a lack of pitch variation that they made you want to throw something. They have made a compelling topic boring and flat, and now their students must make a tremendous effort to stay tuned in.

Activity: Recognizing a Flat Monotone versus Varied Pitch

Speak the following paragraph out loud and do not vary your pitch. Say every single word the same way—in monotone.

> "Hello, everyone. I'm really honored to receive this service award for my team's work with vulnerable children in Appalachia. My amazing student team brought their creativity, skills, and hard work to a high-poverty area of our country that desperately needs attention and support."

It's painful to hear, isn't it? Let's see how much more alive, heartfelt, and authentic the same words can become by modulating the pitch. Say the following paragraph out loud. This time, when a word is in italics, have your pitch be slightly higher, and when a word is in bold, lower your pitch slightly.

> "*Hello*, everyone. I'm *really* honored to receive *this* service award for my team's work with *vulnerable* children in **Appalachia**. My *amazing* student team brought their *creativity*, skills, and **hard work** to a *high*-poverty area of our country that *desperately* needs attention and **support**."

Can you see how much more engaging these sentences are now? If music lacked pitch variation, it would not move us, excite us, soothe us, or make us want to move the way it does. This is also true of language.

Pace

If you wanted to help a child or adult fall asleep, you'd speak softly and at an even and slow pace. On the other hand, if your aim were to pitch your innovative invention to potential funders, you'd want to mix up your pace. To do that, at times you'd speak more quickly and at times you'd speak more slowly.

It is critical that your pacing choices support the story you are sharing. Changing your pace haphazardly and chaotically with no logical motivation has the potential to make you seem frenzied and unfocused. You'll want to look at your content and note where specific pace changes would help emphasize your message.

For example, let's say that you are describing for your audience the moment leading up to when you came up with your groundbreaking idea:

"I had overslept. I jumped out of bed, hopped over my books and guitar, threw on random clothes, ran out of the house, and realized that if I ran faster than I ever had in my life, I would make my bus. I sprinted and made the bus just as the doors were closing, and sat down.

"I was sweaty. My heart was pounding. As I took a moment to collect myself, that's when it hit me. We should be connecting X to Y."

Imagine if you told this entire story at a really slow and even pace. It would lose all excitement. However, if you were to say the first paragraph more quickly and then slow down your pace for the second paragraph, mirroring what you had physically experienced, it would serve the suspense and comedy of your tale. Now explore the story using the pace prompts in parentheses.

"I had overslept. *(quicken pace)* I jumped out of bed, hopped over my books and guitar, threw on random clothes, ran out of the house, and realized that if I ran faster than I ever had in my life, I would make my bus. *(increase pace more)* I sprinted and made the bus just as the doors were closing, and *(start to slow pace)* sat down. *(pause)*

"I was sweaty. My heart was pounding. As I took a moment to collect myself, *(slow pace even more)* that's when it hit me. We should be connecting X to Y."

Can you imagine how these pacing choices could help the audience feel like they were reliving this experience with you?

Pauses

Shows like *Hell's Kitchen* and *American Idol* understand the power of the pause. The hosts know that well-timed pauses build suspense and keep everyone on the edge of their seats to find out who is getting canned and who is getting a contract.

"The winner *(short pause)* of this season's competition *(short pause)* is *(long pause)* Ebony!"

Pauses can:

- Help to highlight a specific point you are making
- Add humor
- Build excitement
- Give the audience a moment to absorb what has just been said
- Allow you to catch your breath

Here's the very beginning of a best-man speech, given by the brother of the groom:

"What can be said of a handsome young man who has moved across the country to seek his fortune away from all he has known? He's forging an exciting new path and making a mark. *(pause)* That's enough about me. Now I'll talk about my brother."

The pause sets up the joke nicely.

Activity: Say the Alphabet Different Ways

This exercise can help you see how much more interesting everything becomes (even something that seems banal, like the alphabet) when you add vocal variety.

1. Say or sing the alphabet out loud.
2. Say the alphabet with as much vocal variety as possible. Spice it up with changes in pitch, pace, pauses, and volume.
3. Say it again as though you were telling a spy thriller with many unexpected and abrupt twists and turns. Utilize various elements of vocal variety from this chapter to vocally build suspense and create an overall mood.

During which version of the alphabet exercise did you feel more alive and present? It's interesting to contemplate that even though you know exactly what letter is coming next, you can still create a fun and surprising ride for yourself and your audience.

Volume

It is critical that everyone in the audience can hear you when you are presenting. (We've already covered breath support and projection, which are very helpful, especially if you are soft-spoken or have a big crowd and no microphone.) That said, varying your volume can make what you are saying more interesting. There may be moments when you want to be more vulnerable. Lower volume can help create a more intimate mood. To add excitement and suspense, you could gradually increase your volume as you build to introducing your new idea.

Aim for the Back of the Room

When you are presenting in a room (big or small) and do not have a microphone, aim to be heard by the people in the back. This will ensure that everyone sitting in the rows in front of them will be able to hear you as well. If you sense that anyone is leaning forward and looking confused, ask them if they can hear you and make the necessary adjustments to your projection based on their answer.

Let's imagine that you are speaking at a fundraiser for an after-school program that had a tremendous impact on your life after you lost your father.

"I remember walking home from school one day when I was ten years old. I had had a great day. I had gotten a one hundred percent on my spelling test and played kickball with my friends during recess. My team won and we gloated about it for the whole afternoon. The sun was shining and I was ready for an afternoon snack of homemade peanut butter cookies.

"But when I got home, I could tell something was very wrong. My mother was sitting on the couch looking stunned and my aunt was crying uncontrollably.

"My uncle pulled me aside and said, 'I'm so sorry, Erik, but your father died of a heart attack at work today.'

"As he hugged me, I felt frozen. Everything seemed unreal."

When we tell a story, we want to bring the audience with us. We want our listeners to experience the story on a visceral level, as though they were living it themselves. Our vocal choices are a critical part of this process. In this example, a loud, upbeat voice would work well to illustrate the happy mood of the first paragraph, which describes a fun day. From the second paragraph onward, speaking in a quieter voice would reflect the seriousness and vulnerability of the very tragic circumstances. This choice would create more intimacy and connection with the audience. You want your listeners to see the world through your eyes, to feel that they were with you at this incredibly significant moment.

(louder volume) "I remember walking home from school one day when I was ten years old. I had had a great day. I had gotten a one hundred percent on my spelling test and played kickball with my friends during recess. My team won and we gloated about it for the whole afternoon. The sun was shining and I was ready for an afternoon snack of homemade peanut butter cookies. *(pause)*

(quieter volume) "But when I got home, I could tell something was very wrong. My mother was sitting on the couch looking stunned and my aunt was crying uncontrollably.

"My uncle pulled me aside and said, 'I'm so sorry, Erik, but your father died of a heart attack at work today.'

"As he hugged me, I felt frozen. *(pause)* Everything seemed unreal."

Activity: Exploring Pitch, Pace, Pauses, and Volume

Let's experiment with various vocal variety options so you can see the range of expression available to you.

1. Say the following tongue twister out loud: "When the winter will withdraw, the weather won't be wild."
2. Say it again and this time mix up your pitch as much as possible. Say some words in a higher voice, some in a lower voice, and some in a pitch somewhere in between.
3. Say it again and this time increase and decrease your pace. Say some parts faster and some parts slower.
4. Say it again while adding some dramatic pauses.
5. Say it again and speak some of the words loudly and some quietly.
6. Say it again and mix up your pitch and add dramatic pauses.
7. Say it again and mix up your pace and add dramatic pauses.
8. Say it again and mix up your volume and add dramatic pauses.
9. Say it again and do all of the above!

Another Useful Time to Increase Your Volume

Your choice of volume can help your audience to know when you are addressing a new topic within your talk. I encourage my clients to speak more loudly, with fresh energy, when they begin discussing a new subject. When a PowerPoint presentation is part of the show, I tell them, "Each slide is like a brand-new day. Bring a burst of fresh energy to each new slide."

Following is a very short presentation about sloths, our smiley and zen friends who live in the jungles of Central and South America. The bold print indicates where to come in with increased volume.

"Approximately sixty percent of a sloth's life is spent resting. When they do move, they move very slowly and go no faster than one mile per hour.

"Not only do sloths' bodies move slowly through the treetops, but their digestive process is also very leisurely. It can take their system an entire month to digest a single leaf."

Activity: Make a Story Better by Adding Vocal Variety

Say the following story out loud and explore all of the ways you could make this story vocally interesting. Consider when you could add dramatic pauses, increase or slow down your pace for suspense, mix up your pitch, and modulate your volume to create a compelling story.

"I had had a really rough week. Work was incredibly frustrating. No one was listening to my ideas or respecting my skills or my time.

"I really needed to blow off steam. I decided to go for a run.

"I walked to the nearby woods and started running. My anger was fueling me and I started running faster and faster. No one else was around, so I decided to get rid of more stress by yelling.

"Ahhhhhh! I hate my job!

"Why don't you idiots listen to me?

"I am more qualified than most of you!

"After shouting a bit longer, I grew quiet. Yelling at colleagues who were nowhere in sight felt cathartic. Still running, I was feeling more empowered than I had in a long while. I was feeling strong, bold, and free. Maybe it was time for a change. I could update my resume pretty quickly, I could—

"Smack!

"I wiped out. I had skidded on some wet leaves and ripped both of my knees open. My chocolate chip Clif Bar went flying, as did my brand-new iPhone. I yelled some choice words and then just sat there in my misery, feeling totally drained.

"I don't know how long I sat there. But suddenly I heard some noises behind me in the woods.

"At first I couldn't tell if the rustling sounds were being made by a human or an animal. But when I did finally catch a glimpse of what was making the noise, I saw that it was a bear. A bear with her two little cubs. Probably a very protective mother bear.

"This was not good."

Real-World Example:
A Young Woman Uses Vocal Variety and Creativity to Turn the Everyday Into Art

Recently I taught a workshop to a group of high school students who attend Raw Art Works, an amazing after-school arts program in Lynn, Massachusetts. Its mission: "RAW ignites the desire to create and the confidence to succeed in our youth." For some of the workshop we focused on how to integrate vocal variety into storytelling. I asked for a volunteer to describe to the group how to make a peanut butter and jelly sandwich, and to make this activity sound like an amazing adventure. What the young female volunteer did in response to those simple instructions was really incredible. Using a spoken-word style, Sam, my volunteer, described the ingredients and her decision to have toast. She added drama by sharing her slight hesitation about which utensil to use to get the peanut butter out of the jar, and how she arrived at her choice. Sam slowed down when she shared about smooooooothing the peanut butter onto the bread, and then moving to the jaaaaaaaaam. She concluded by adding, "I am [pause] eating."

Sam elevated this simple task to art. By using dramatic pauses, inhabiting each moment, and varying her pace, pitch, and volume, she made this act soulful, existential, and deep.

I asked the other students what made the story memorable. They mentioned the pauses, her choice of words, the way she said specific words, her details, and her tone. One young woman said that she could picture Sam making this sandwich wearing a beret and little glasses. Someone else chimed in that they could imagine incense. It was a great example of how a creative use of language can transport us to another time and place.

Choose a Simple Story for Practice

When you are learning a new public speaking skill, such as adding vocal variety, it can be helpful to practice with a story (making a sandwich, doing dishes) that you don't have to think about too deeply.

Avoiding Filler Words

Being attentive to your breathing and intentionally choosing a variety of vocal options to express your thoughts and ideas will help your presentation sound natural and engaging. Now let's think about how to avoid filler words, which can be distracting to your audience. Filler words are those words that habitually come out when you feel you need to be talking but have not yet thought through what you are saying. Examples:

- "Umm, I, **like**, went to UNC for undergrad and I, **like**, learned a lot about bio."
- "I got my graduate degree in social work and, **you know**, want to help parents who are struggling."
- "I am studying electrical engineering and I **kinda** want to apply that to robotics."
- "I'm here to help **you guys** with training."

Many people who come to see me are aware that they are adding filler words but don't know how to get rid of them. Sometimes they don't realize just how often they have been including them in their sentences. Let's review some common filler words.

Ummmmmm...

I have observed a couple of patterns with *um*. The first is using *um* at the beginning of a sentence. This is a significant problem when a person is asked a question. They feel pressured to answer right away, as though they are on a game show and must hit the buzzer before the other contestants. They don't have their answer thought out just yet, but they feel a need to start talking. Here comes the *um*!

"Tim, what are your thoughts about the new marketing strategy?"
"Ummmmm, I think, um, it's interesting."

It's perfectly fine to give yourself time to be thoughtful. I would rather have you get your thoughts together in silence than frantically blurt out an *ummmm* followed by several incoherent sentences.

Another common *um* habit is to use it as a transition word between sentences, rather than being comfortable with a pause.

Activity: Take the *Um* Challenge!

You may not even realize when or how often you are using the word *um*. This activity will help bring your awareness to this very popular filler word.

1. Enlist a friend or colleague with whom you feel comfortable. Let them know that you are trying to eliminate *um* from your vocabulary.
2. Have them ask you ten random questions about a topic that you know well. It can be your taste in music, your favorite Netflix series, your childhood, your first job—anything you can talk about easily will work. Your partner in this task will raise their hand each time you say "um." This in itself will help your awareness increase, which is half the battle.
3. Your goal is to not start answering their questions until you are ready. Give yourself the luxury of time to consider your words before speaking.

4. If your friend or colleague noticed that you use other filler words—*you guys, kinda, sorta, like, you know*—you can play the game again, focusing on one of those.

Kinda, Sorta, Maybe

I have a theory that people add the words *kinda, sorta,* and *maybe* to make their language seem more casual and conversational. I may or may not be right, but I do know that adding these words has the potential to lessen the impact of what you are saying.

Here are some patterns I have noticed with these particular words:

- **They can indicate shyness:** Consider this introduction: "I am so happy to be giving a wedding toast for my buddy, Brad. We've kinda been best friends since fourth grade." Here I think that the person giving the toast is feeling shy about definitely claiming that Brad and he are besties. It would be more polished to say, "Brad has been one of my closest friends since fourth grade."

- **They can confuse your message:** If you say, "These graphs show that there has been sort of an uptick in sales," I imagine that the uptick in sales has not been very strong. A clearer way to express this would be, "These graphs show that there has been a small uptick in sales."

- **They can undermine your authority:** If you're worried about appearing bossy, you may insert the word *maybe* to soften your message. For example: "Maybe I could present second and maybe you could go first? That order makes sense, because you are better at explaining why we are doing this project, and I love sharing what our specific plans and steps are." Or, "Maybe if we raised the money, we could fund the after-school program so that it would not need to close its doors." Here are alternative and more confident ways to express the same things. "You are better at explaining why we are doing this project, and I love sharing what our specific plans and steps are. So I suggest that you present our 'why' first and I present our vision and 'how' second. What are your thoughts?" Or, "If we raise the funds, this important after-school program can continue to help kids thrive and grow."

You're working so hard to infuse your message with passion and information—don't undermine your efforts with these throwaway words that could make people question you. It's okay to be an authority when you're speaking in public.

The Word *Like*

The word *like* is, like, everywhere! Please use it when you are fond of someone or something or when you say similes such as "crazy like a fox." But using it frequently as a filler word can make you sound unprofessional and immature. Similar to other filler words, it dilutes your message by cluttering up your sentences.

In a professional setting peppering your sentences with *like* is not going to serve you. Heighten your awareness around this habit (revisit the "Take the *Um* Challenge!" activity) and see if you can insert it less.

Real-World Example:
Dimitrous Adds Belly Breathing and Nixes Filler Words

In the following example, Dimitrous learns how proper breathing support from the diaphragm helps him to calm down, slow down, and improve his vocal quality and storytelling.

Dimitrous is a successful entrepreneur with a great passion for his work and a lot of charisma. He came to me because he wanted to polish his public speaking skills. Dimitrous, like many people, had a few habitual filler words that regularly crept in while he was speaking. He also would attempt to say too many words all on one breath, which would result in "vocal fry" (we'll discuss this later in this chapter) at the ends of his sentences. This is a very common habit. It lessens the quality of the sound of your voice, and as you run out of air, your body starts to get uncomfortable and you can feel shortness of breath. This can lead to a sense of panic.

First, we worked on some diaphragmatic breathing (belly breathing) exercises. Dimitrous noted that the exercises helped him to feel more relaxed, grounded, and clear-minded. To practice supporting his words in a new way, I asked him to tell me how to make a BLT sandwich, using only short sentences, fully supported by his breath. As he went through the steps, his vocal quality was overall better and he was no longer running out of air by the end of each sentence. The story was a bit slower, more interesting, and fun.

Slowing down also enabled Dimitrous to become aware of when his habitual filler words, *you know*, became part of the story. With practice, he started to be able to refrain from saying these words when he was unsure of what to say next. As a result, he became more comfortable with taking pauses. Not only did this give Dimitrous time to take a breath and help him to avoid filler words, but pauses also made his storytelling more interesting.

Other Vocal Issues to Avoid

Filler words are probably the most common issue people face. But upspeak and vocal fry are two other potential problems that you can avoid if you are aware of them as you practice.

Upspeak

Upspeak, or uptalk, describes a rising intonation at the end of a sentence. This way of speaking, when done repeatedly, makes it sound like every sentence is a question. If every sentence you are saying is really a question, then upspeak makes sense. But if very few of your sentences are questions, then it is unhelpful.

Here is an example of what upspeak sounds like: "My name is Jessica? I live in Columbus? I went to Ohio State?"

Upspeak does not help the speaker to exude confidence. It may be borne from an effort to be inclusive and kind; the intention underneath may be to ask your audience, "Are you with me?" Nonetheless, it's better to own your sentences: "My name is Jessica. I live in Columbus and I went to Ohio State."

Vocal Fry

Vocal fry is the lowest register of the voice. If someone is speaking with vocal fry, their voice sounds raspy, scratchy, or creaky. If you go to *YouTube* and search for "vocal fry," you will find numerous videos demonstrating it, including quite a few clips of Kim Kardashian. I first learned about it in grad school from a singing teacher who said it occurred when there wasn't enough breath support. According to Johns Hopkins Medicine, here's what is happening: "When you speak, your vocal cords naturally close to create vibrations as air passes between them. Like a piano or guitar string, these vibrations produce sound (your voice). When you breathe, your vocal cords are relaxed and open to let air pass through freely, which doesn't produce any sound.

When you use vocal fry, you relax your vocal cords but do not increase the amount of air you're pushing past your vocal cords, which produces slower vibrations and ultimately results in the lower creaky sound."

Vocal fry has been in the news quite a bit recently. Women are getting a bad rap for using vocal fry, though men use it as well. Is it bad? Vocal fry does not harm your voice. But if it is getting in the way of you being understood when you are presenting, then it's time to choose another option. Some people find it grating to listen to. Personally, I think people have better vocal quality and are easier to understand when they do not have vocal fry, so I encourage my clients to avoid it by making sure they have proper breath support by using their diaphragm.

A Natural Way to Treat a Sore Throat

It's a bummer to wake up with a sore throat when you need to present. You can soothe your sore throat by gargling with warm salt water. Simply stir ½ teaspoon of salt into a full glass of warm water and gargle. This will reduce swelling and clean your throat. Other ways to keep your voice healthy include staying hydrated, being sure to warm up your voice before presenting, avoiding cigarettes, and avoiding clearing your throat.

When You Have an Accent

I have coached many clients for whom English is their second or third language. If they have an accent, they are often concerned about sounding different and are worried that they are not always understood. They feel anxious when they can't always remember the English word they want to say right away.

When Accents Do Not Affect Audience Comprehension

When clients with an accent share their thoughts with me, I start to get a sense of how easy they are to understand. Often, their accent is in no way making it hard for me to understand them. But I can see that they are self-conscious about it, which detracts from their confidence. In this case, I reassure them that they do not need to worry. Their accent, though apparent, is not getting in the way, unless they get too focused on it and become self-conscious. I also tell them that I will make a point to let them know if I hear any pronunciation errors, so they can begin to trust themselves fully. I encourage them to instead embrace that they have an accent.

When Accents Do Affect Audience Comprehension

If your accent is making it difficult for your audience to understand you, you have many options at your disposal:

- **Consult with a professional coach.** There are coaches who specialize in accent reduction and can help you make the changes in pronunciation and cadence that will allow you to be understood more easily.
- **Take a conversational English class.** This type of class can help you be more fluid with your pronunciation and word choices.
- **Take advantage of self-study materials.** There are online courses, books, and apps that can guide you.
- **Ask a trusted friend or colleague for help.** In the absence of using a professional coach, you could enlist a friend or colleague to help discern understandability and pronunciation errors. Often there are just a few specific sounds that are challenging, or you may be in the habit of emphasizing certain words or syllables that make your sentences harder to understand. Your friend or colleague can help you identify these and guide you so that won't need to repeat yourself to be understood.

When You Can't Recall a Word

When a client has difficulty recalling an exact English word, I tell them that English is my first and only language, and sometimes I can't come up with the exact word I am looking for. I also share a story about a grad student from Mali who took my public speaking class. Ayo was a confident man with a lot of presence and passion. On the final day of class Ayo gave a presentation. At one point he paused, clearly searching for the right word. What was beautiful about this moment was that instead of getting stressed or self-conscious, he delighted in the wait and trusted that the word would come to him, which it did. To the audience it seemed like Ayo was honoring his story and us by trying to find the exact right word to describe what he was saying. He was like an artist patiently looking for the exact right shade of blue to finish painting a sky. His pause also added some suspense leading up to the word. It was a great and memorable moment, with no anxiety or apology. So don't stress about forgetting and searching for a word. Try to wait and see if the word comes (it often does—as with Ayo). If the word remains elusive, you could say the equivalent word in your native language and then define it for your listeners.

Using a Microphone

There are several different kinds of microphones you may encounter when presenting. In the following sections I'll describe each type of microphone, note when you would potentially use it, and share tips for having a good relationship with the mic.

Handheld Microphone

This traditional type of microphone is often used for toasts and Q&As. Here are some tips for sounding your best on a handheld mic:

- **Hold it firmly.** A microphone's job is to amplify sound. It will do this when you speak, but it will also amplify the sounds your hands make if you excessively handle the mic. Be sure to hold the mic firmly to cut down on these unnecessary sounds. (This is also why it's better to use a mic inside rather than outside, since when outside it will pick up the sounds of wind and traffic.)

- **Hold the mic approximately 6 inches away from your mouth.** If you hold it closer than that, the mic will pick up too many sounds, and if you hold it farther away, your voice won't be amplified well enough. It's best to angle it toward your mouth and consistently hold it there while speaking. You can hold your script or gesture with your other hand.
- **Consider holding it for other speakers.** If there is only one mic and you are the host but have people asking questions or giving short answers, it can be better for you to hold it (properly) for other speakers. Otherwise, your audience will probably hear lots of extra noise during the mic handoff and as the other contributors try to figure out how to hold the mic for themselves.
- **If you are not speaking, keep the mic near (but not touching) your chest.** This will prevent it from picking up lots of ambient sound. If you point the mic at a floor monitor or loudspeaker, you will get feedback, which is really unpleasant.
- **Practice!** If it is possible, rehearse with the mic you'll be using before your event. Learn how to turn it on and off, what its sensitivity level is, and how to tell if it needs new batteries. When you are done speaking, be sure to turn it off.

Lavalier Microphone

A lavalier mic, or lav, is a very small mic that is typically affixed to the collar of your shirt. (It is also called a clip-on mic, lapel mic, body mic, or personal mic.) It is either wireless or battery powered. If the latter is the case, the battery pack will attach to the inside of your pants or skirt waistband. Then a wire with a tiny mic on the end will go under your clothes and emerge at your neckline. The mic usually has a clip on it to secure it to your clothing. Film and TV actors use these every day on set, but they are hidden in their clothes. In public speaking circumstances it's absolutely fine if your mic can be seen.

Speakers often use lav mics at large events and during interviews. An advantage to this type of mic is that your hands are totally free to hold your notes and gesture.

Here are some tips for working with lav mics:

- **Try it first.** Test the mic before using it to see if it is affixed in a good location and not rubbing against your clothing.
- **Learn how it works.** Make sure you know how to turn your lav mic on and off. It is so lightweight that it can be easy to forget that you are wearing it. You want to be sure to turn your lav off before you use the restroom or have any conversations that you would prefer the world not hear.

Become a Lav Mic Expert

If you're going to be using a lav mic frequently, you might want to become even more proficient with one. For more tips and instructions, check out www.videomaker.com/article/c04/19290-how-to-properly-use-a-wireless-lavalier-microphone.

Stationary Microphone

A stationary mic is a microphone that sits on a podium or table. These mics are often used for events like graduation speeches and keynote addresses. They are also utilized frequently for panel discussions and podcasts. Here are some tips for working with one of these:

- **Test its power ahead of time.** If possible, rehearse with this mic to figure out how close to (or far from) it you need to be to achieve the volume you want.
- **Speak directly into the mic.** The mic should be set up at an optimal height for you to do this (i.e., not be so low that speaking into it is awkward). Obviously, it is critical that people hear you, so do what you need to do to speak into it. You may need to adjust it so that it is pointing at your mouth. To avoid annoying feedback, adjust by the neck, not the mic itself.
- **Speak approximately 8 to 10 inches away from the mic.** At this distance you won't be spitting into the mic and you'll have a little bit of freedom of movement. That said, keep your mouth directed toward the mic.

Wireless Headset

One of the advantages of using a headset mic is that the mic stays the same distance from your mouth at all times without rubbing against your clothing. Similar to the lav mic, your hands are totally free to gesture, write on a whiteboard, or advance your slides.

These types of mics are often used for speaking engagements, leading exercise workouts like spinning or boot camps, and for people who spend a lot of their time on the phone—such as sales representatives or customer service reps.

A few cool features of headsets:

- They have high-quality speakers, and you can determine the position of the speaker over your ear.
- Many have amplifiers that allow you to set the volume and tone.

- Many headsets are able to block out background sounds using noise-canceling technology.
- What's great about the position of the headset's mic is that it can pick up your voice while at the same time avoiding your facial movements and any associated sounds.

Boom Mic

A boom mic is a microphone that is attached to a very long pole. It is usually covered by what is called a "blimp," which helps to filter out the sound of wind. These are used for TV and film, and are held strategically by tech professionals. When working with a boom mic, you will not be responsible for anything except following whatever directions you receive regarding volume and where to direct your voice.

PART THREE

The Presentation

Parts One and Two shared strategies for building your confidence emotionally, mentally, and physically. You learned how to let go of unhelpful beliefs that no longer serve you, develop a compelling voice, handle nerves, and focus on your audience's needs above all else. In Part Three I will address three other important components: crafting your message, preparing for your specific setting, and engaging with your audience.

In Chapter 5 I'll explain what you need to understand about your audience and why knowing "what's in it for them" is important. I'll cover how to write a compelling talk, with an engaging beginning, memorable stories, and creative use of language. You'll read about how to rehearse your presentation, and how and when to memorize. You'll discover what makes slides work for you rather than against you and how to get helpful feedback from your community. In Chapter 6 you'll learn how to best prepare—by understanding what is and what is not in your control and also the importance of positive visualization and self-care. I'll share strategies for handling different speaking scenarios, from networking events to wedding toasts to podcasts. The final chapter of the book, Chapter 7, will address how to create a great experience for your audience. You'll receive insights on how your intentions affect the crowd and why empathy and gratitude are important. You'll also learn how to stay in the moment and how to get back on track if you go off course.

CHAPTER 5

Creating Your Talk—
The Nitty-Gritty of Writing
and Rehearsing

How do you begin writing your talk, anyway? This chapter will explore how to brainstorm, how to organize your ideas, and how to express them creatively in your own voice. You'll learn how to get and keep your audience's attention from the start and how to inspire them to take action. We'll dig into how your slides are not a crutch but rather a witty sidekick. I'll also cover how to rehearse with your easy-to-read script, notes, or outline, so you can provide a transformative experience for your audience and maybe even get some laughs—when you want them.

Who, Why, What, How, When

That's right—let's start with the basics. To write a talk, you need to know:

- **Who** you are writing it for
- **Why** you are writing it
- **What** you need to get across—the problem(s) and how you are going to solve it (or them)
- **How** to best explain the problem(s) and solution(s) using stories, examples, ideas, facts, figures, and/or images
- **When** and what you want people to do after they listen to and see all that you share

Identifying this key information will help you write content that's specific, relevant, interesting, and motivating for your audience.

Understanding Your Audience

Learning as much as you can about your audience will assist you in determining how to strategically get your message across. The more knowledge you have about them, the more intelligently you can shape your approach.

Here is a list of questions to ask yourself or others about your audience when preparing for your next talk. Even if your answers reveal information that may seem negative, it is better to know it in advance rather than find it out as you begin speaking, or after the fact.

- Roughly how many people are expected to attend?
- Is everyone in the audience at the same level in terms of knowledge and expertise in regard to your subject? If not, what are their different levels?
- Is there any jargon you will need to explain?
- Are your attendees choosing to attend or are they required to attend (i.e., do they want to be there)?
- What are all of the possible reasons they will attend?
- Are there any belief systems about your topic that may create resistance? If so, what are they? For example, if you are giving a talk about healthy habits, part of your audience may believe "I'm way too busy to add exercising to my overpacked schedule."
- If there are belief systems that may create resistance, what creative strategies could you try to help your audience reconsider their way of thinking?
- Are there any cultural perspectives that you need to take into account? The answers to this question may influence how you dress, what humor you choose, and how you shape your overall approach.
- What does your audience stand to gain from listening to you?
- What time of day is your talk? Are there reasons your audience may be tired (perhaps they are either just waking up or tired after a long day)? Could they be oversaturated with information (say, if you have the last slot of a weeklong conference)?
- If you anticipate they will be tired, how can you creatively address this (and not feel like you are cursed with the worst slot)?

While preparing, you may become aware of possible perceptions or misperceptions that could create resistance to your talk. It's important to directly or indirectly address these during your presentation. This will go a long way toward helping your audience to feel seen and understood. This will assist you with winning their trust and opening their minds to consider your point of view.

Once you get a clearer picture of who your audience is, your strategy for how to reach them will become clearer. Your "who" may also help inspire your "why." Once you get a sense of their perspectives and openness (or lack thereof), the reasons your talk is valuable may become clearer.

> ## Does Your Audience Want to Be There?
>
> One of the most critical questions is "Do the participants want to be at your talk?" Determining how potentially receptive or unreceptive your audience will be to your message is a crucial step. If attendees are motivated to attend only because they are required to, you need to find a way to engage them as early as possible, so that they are open and receptive to your message. You want them to *want* to be there.

Real-World Example:
Jackie Figures Out Her Audience

Here is a great example of how your "who" can help determine your "how." One of my clients, Jackie, came to see me to help her prepare for a large conference in the South. Her topic—how healthy eating habits could help prevent or delay Alzheimer's, a devastating degenerative brain disease. Jackie had some fascinating and hopeful new research to share. Her goal was to motivate her audience to change their eating habits for themselves and model the change for others (family members, patients, and/or clients). I asked her some questions about her audience:

1. **Who would be in her audience?** There would be occupational, speech, and physical therapists; nurses; social workers; mental health providers; nursing home administrators; family caregivers; students; and, very importantly, seniors.
2. **Did the attendees want to hear what she was going to say?** The attendees had chosen to attend, which indicated that they were interested in learning all they could about this heartbreaking illness. Okay, good.
3. **Was there a strong desire to change? Would audience members necessarily want to commit to making small changes to their eating habits over time as a result of listening to a ninety-minute talk?** The jury was out. The conference was in a state where many people struggled with poor eating habits and obesity. There was definitely a deep need for new habits. If audience members didn't start with a strong desire to change, it was up to Jackie to do all she could to create one.

Here are some other details that Jackie took note of as she learned about her audience:

- Some attendees would be open to learning about healthy eating and its connection to brain health, while others would also be convinced by the research to immediately start making small changes in their diets.
- For some, though the research might seem compelling, changing eating habits would not be appealing. Healthy eating would sound like a total drag and not yummy. Images of weird, bleak, unsatisfying meals would dance through their heads.
- Some may erroneously believe that healthy eating is always more expensive than fast food.

- People also identify with different foods and different brands. Some people identify with Dunkin' Donuts coffee, whereas others identify with Starbucks. Some folks may have a warm relationship with kale and quinoa. Others may see those as trendy hipster foods, which could be a turnoff.
- The word *diet* has negative connotations for many. It's a charged word that often evokes thoughts of deprivation, restrictions, judgment, and failure.

We needed to find a way to get as much of the audience's buy-in as we could. Just because an audience comprehended something intellectually didn't mean they would be inspired to commit to change. Jackie needed to provide compelling reasons as to why audience members would want to jump on board.

Jackie's first goal was to open their minds. She wanted to show how they could avoid a really bad thing, Alzheimer's, by adopting new habits and foods that were good for them—and tasted good too! During the first few minutes of her presentation she clarified how to think about the word *diet* in the context of her presentation. Jackie wanted them to think of a diet as guidelines for a lifestyle—one that would potentially give them a sharper memory, better thinking skills, and a higher quality of life. Jackie then described brain-healthy foods that sounded delicious and indulgent—like irresistible, creamy chocolate mousse (surprise! one of the ingredients is avocados!). She went on to compare the brain to the engine of a car, such as a Ferrari or a Porsche. Jackie explained that the higher the quality of the fuel you put in, the better and longer the car would run. She then described delicious, top-grade fuel for the brain, including legumes and beans. To add some humor, for the segment about beans we created a comedic poem inspired by "Beans, beans, they're good for your heart. The more you eat them, the more you fart." So, very early on in her talk Jackie achieved four goals:

1. She enticed her audience with a surprisingly yummy, healthy dessert to negate the belief that all healthy food was a bummer.
2. She gave the word *diet* a new spin, so people could stay open when they heard the word.
3. She mentioned sexy sports cars in her analogy, to help people respect their brains and bodies in a new way.
4. Last, but most definitely not least, Jackie used humor to give her talk about a serious disease moments of lightness and fun.

This approach helped the audience feel that she was on their team, talking *with* them instead of judging and lecturing them on how they must eat lima beans and drink cod liver oil every day...or else.

Activity: Create an Outline for Your Talk by Determining Who, Why, What, How, When

This activity will help you organize your thoughts about your audience, your motivation, your topic, and how you will creatively get your information across.

Brainstorm

Here are some ideas to jump-start your brainstorming process:

1. List all of the different groups of people that could be in your audience. Include what you understand their knowledge of your topic to be.

2. List all of the reasons why this talk would benefit your audience. Which one is most compelling to you?
3. List the problem(s) you will be addressing.
4. List your solution(s) to these problems.
5. List any resistance—intellectual and/or emotional—that you anticipate.
6. List any parameters you have: Do you have a time limit or a slide limit? Is it important that you avoid using jargon? Is anyone else sharing on a related topic?
7. Read over your lists and see what stories or analogies come to mind that would creatively express:

   - Why your talk is important to your audience
   - A description of the problem
   - A description of your solution

8. Say each of those stories and analogies out loud to yourself. It may help to record yourself or take notes for future reference.
9. Which stories and analogies (more on these later in this chapter) best illustrate the points you would like to make?
10. Draft an outline. See what works for the beginning, middle, and end of your talk. You can always rearrange your ideas if you are inspired to do so.
11. Based on your loose outline, do a messy run-through of your talk out loud. Take note of which parts flow and which parts need some transitional help. Jot down any new thoughts.
12. Keep playing with your talk until you are happy with the order and the flow.
13. Now it's time to refine what you've got. Let your original lists guide this process, and cut whatever doesn't serve your goals.

Refine Your Content

The who/why/what/how/when exercise should help you come up with a lot of content. If you find that you now have a bunch of quality material but have lost your way in terms of structure, try this exercise. Challenge yourself to do a five-minute version of your talk, and then a one-minute version. You will be forced to distill your ideas to their simplest form. And you'll have a better sense of how to get from point A to point B to point C and so on. This will give you editing and structuring ideas for the full talk.

It's Okay to Be Messy

Let yourself be messy with your process, and see what your research and imagination bring to you. You may have many rough drafts, but that does not mean you are a bad writer. Just start. It is okay if it is awkward and your grammar and spelling are terrible. You'll clean it all up later.

Add a Call to Action

At this point you have written (or at least outlined) a talk that helps your audience understand something more deeply. If you have written a toast, your audience will learn some new things about the person or people being toasted. If you have created a pitch for your new invention, your audience will see what problems your invention will solve and how you will bring your plan to fruition. It's now time to take the next step: making a call to action. At the end of your talk you need to let people know what action to take.

Impart a Sense of Urgency

To inspire your audience to take action you need to make sure there is a sense of urgency. You want them to feel a deep need to do something—now. People have so much going on in their lives and at work; plus, many marketers and organizations are trying to get their attention at every turn. To cut through the noise, you need to ignite a fire in your audience's bellies to take your call to action seriously. Your talk needs to be structured and delivered in such a way that it gives the audience steps toward your call to action.

This call to action could take several forms:

- If you pitched a new idea, you could ask for funding, resource support, and/or partnerships.
- If you made a toast, you can ask people to raise their glasses in congratulations.
- If you raised awareness on a topic like suicide prevention, you could give instructions as to how to talk to someone who may be suicidal.

Here's what a call to action could look like if you were wrapping up a presentation on suicide prevention:

"Thank you so much for giving your attention to this very important and difficult subject. I know we covered a lot of ground. After you leave here, I hope you'll approach anyone talking about suicide in a proactive way. Don't be afraid to ask if they are thinking about taking their own life. You're not suggesting it by bringing it up, and you might be able to help them. I will now pass out materials that will help you know where to go for support if you are ever in this situation. Again, suicide is the tenth leading cause of death in the US. Thank you for doing what you can to help to prevent suicide."

Incorporate Your Own Style Into Your Writing

The content of your speech is clearly very important, but so are other aspects that contribute to a public speaking experience's success: your personality, humor, and ability to connect with your audience. These components combine to create your particular style of speaking. Along these lines, to create a great talk you need to figure out how you are going to:

- Immediately get your audience's attention
- Paint verbal pictures of the problem(s) and solutions(s)—using stories, examples, ideas, facts, figures, and images in the most interesting and relevant way possible
- Think of compelling analogies to get your points across
- Use humor to get your message across
- Close out your speech on a strong note

The following sections will delve into each of these areas.

Begin Strongly—Unique Beginnings

In Chapter 1 you learned that public speaking is not about you. This feels truer when you engage with the audience by asking them to consider a question or statement. Your compelling question or bold sentence needs to be relevant to your topic. It's great if it can cut right to the problem or cause you are trying to get your audience to care about. If you first win their hearts and open their minds, their actions and investments will potentially follow.

Open Boldly

"Pit bulls make great pets."
That sentence got your attention, right? How about this question:

"What animal is living freely in the big city of Mumbai, India, potentially saving the city money and protecting the citizens?" (Answer: leopards!)

When you start your presentation with a sentence or question that is strong, unique, and attention-getting, you wake up your audience and make them curious to hear more. Many clients have told me that the first few minutes of a presentation are the worst for them. That's when their heart is racing, their hands are shaking, and they are scared they will go blank. Once they get through the first few minutes, they settle down.

Beginning with a powerful statement or compelling question has the potential to immediately establish rapport with your audience. It also puts the focus on them.

"Who in this room likes feeling nervous?"

This is often how I begin my workshops. I usually hear some nervous laughter; a few folks say, "Yeah, right." One or two brave souls sometimes raise their hands and share that they like the rush of adrenaline and thrive on the challenge of getting out of their comfort zone. This interaction leads to a great discussion about when folks are able to embrace nervous energy (when on roller coasters or when doing intense sports, like skydiving) and when it feels too difficult (when public speaking, when public speaking, and, oh, when public speaking). My question wakes people up, gets them thinking and talking, and begins the lesson.

To avoid opening an overflowing can of worms, don't ask open-ended questions. "What is the meaning of life?" is a wonderful, profound question, but it could derail your talk. It's better to go with a question that has a yes-or-no answer, or a multiple-choice question with answers that you provide. The audience can respond by raising their hands at your prompting.

Say you are a shark conservationist; the following questions could help get an audience thinking:

"How many humans do sharks kill per year? *(pause)*
   "With a show of hands, how many people think that on a yearly basis sharks kill fifty people? One hundred? Three hundred?
   "The answer? Sharks kill approximately one person in the US and fewer than six people worldwide per year, according to Mother Nature Network.

"Here's another question: how many sharks do humans kill each year? *(pause)*

"With a show of hands, how many people think that on a yearly basis humans kill fifty sharks? *(pause)* A thousand? *(pause)* Three thousand? *(pause)*

"Also, according to Mother Nature Network, humans kill approximately 100 million sharks per year. You are more likely to be killed by a mosquito or a hippo than a shark."

Do you see how these questions and answers have the potential to help the audience think about sharks differently? They may even start to feel for them and see the value in protecting them, all within a few minutes.

The key to asking questions during a presentation is to choose questions whose answers will reveal unexpected, cool, or really disturbing information that connects to your motivation for giving the presentation.

Let's imagine that the shark conservationist speaker ultimately wants to raise money for her organization and also raise awareness about the need to protect sharks. She will have more success if she is able to inspire the audience to care about sharks, rather than fear and despise them.

1. Her mission—to raise money
2. Her "why"—sharks need protecting
3. Her "how"—getting the audience to care about and respect sharks, by telling stories and sharing information that will change how they view sharks

Aim your question(s) or bold statements toward the why and/or the how. That's what will make an impact.

Open by Connecting Your Audience to Their Own Experience

Another way to engage your audience right from the start is to connect them to their own experience. Here's an example:

"Take a moment to close your eyes. Think back to when you were in middle school. See if you can remember the teachers you had, who your friends were, and how you felt about yourself and your family. Now visualize what you did after school.

"Did you go home and watch television all afternoon? Did you play a sport? Did you go to an after-school program?

"Whatever experience you had, how did it make you feel? Did you have fun? Did you feel safe? Supported?"

This specific exercise helps the audience to see what they valued or disliked about their early teen years. If the speaker is trying to raise money for an after-school program in a dangerous area, he has helped his audience to start to identify with the kids who would be served by such a program. Or he has helped them to see how fortunate they were to have what they had, and he will hopefully be able to encourage them to be generous so others can have a similar experience.

Storytelling—Paint Pictures with Your Words

A picture may be worth a thousand words, but a great story is made up of a thousand pictures. You need to paint pictures for your audience to fully engage them mentally and emotionally. A well-chosen and well-told story, when woven into your talk, can do a lot of heavy lifting for you. Stories that capture the imaginations and hearts of your audience members will transport them from their worlds to yours. Full engagement leads to receptivity to new ideas, vision, and solutions. This is when transformation happens.

You may be thinking, *But I'm not good at storytelling! Kim, my cousin, she's really good. She's funny and smart. Me, not so much.*

Remy, the furry little chef in the animated film *Ratatouille*, believed that "anyone can cook." Well, I believe that anything can be framed to be interesting, engaging, and memorable. Don't believe me? *Seinfeld*, the hugely popular 1990s sitcom, was described as a show about "nothing," and 76.3 million viewers watched the series finale. If "nothing" can win Emmy Awards, then imagine how great your story of substance has the potential to be.

Read the following two examples and see which one affects you more deeply.

1. "I am raising money for at-risk youth, a very worthy cause."
2. "I'm going to tell you about a young boy I know named Samuel. He is thirteen years old and lives with his grandmother because his mother is in prison and his dad was killed during a robbery. He lives in a housing project and his older brother is in a local gang. Samuel's grandmother waitresses at several restaurants and is usually not home when he gets out of school. He misses his mom and has started hanging out with his brother and his brother's friends. If he had a Boys & Girls Club nearby, he would have a better alternative for his afternoons and potentially a better future."

Do you see how this story helps to captivate your imagination? The term *at-risk youth* is descriptive but not as powerful as a short story describing the vulnerability of a child in a challenging family situation, living in a dangerous neighborhood.

Here's an example of a near-missed opportunity: I was leading a workshop for healthcare providers. During the first part of our time together, a woman spoke about her inspiring work building the healthcare system in an African country. She discussed the approach her organization was taking and cited some statistics. She also told us that people in that area were suspicious of hospitals and doctors. During the Q&A, one of the questions prompted her to tell us a very sad story about a woman whose health was at risk. A doctor who was visiting her home had recommended that she seek medical attention at the hospital immediately. The ill woman would not speak to the doctor directly. Her in-laws spoke on her behalf and told the doctor she did not need to go. Without proper treatment, the woman died several days after the doctor's visit. This tragic event represented a deep need for the limited beliefs—suspicions—about healthcare and doctors to change.

I later asked the group what was most memorable about the woman's presentation. Many chimed in that they were so struck by the story about the woman who had tragically died. I felt the same way. I then pointed out that we could have easily not heard the story because it was not part of the official presentation; it only came up because of a particular question during the Q&A. Telling that story would have been a very powerful way for her to start the talk. The audience would have been emotionally invested and would also have understood the obstacles that the woman's team in the field was facing.

Activity: Mine Your Story for Details

One way to make your stories rich and multilayered is to focus on the smaller details within them. This exercise will help you think about an experience and break it down into smaller parts, focusing on feelings and sensations.

1. Choose a seemingly mundane recent experience. It could be commuting to work, cleaning your home, or taking your dog for a walk.
2. Describe this experience out loud, moment to moment, as though you are reliving it. Bring the story to life, if only for yourself and the furniture around you. Include:

- What you experience in terms of your senses, using descriptive adjectives to explain what you see, hear, and so on (cruel humidity, heavenly air conditioning)
- What feelings come up
- What you discover, realize, or remember

3. What parts of your story stood out to you? Why? If you need an objective listener, ask a trusted friend or colleague to listen to your story and answer these questions.

Take note of what types of details were most memorable. See if you can apply this lesson to relevant stories at your next public speaking opportunity.

Using Descriptive Analogies

Another way your personal style can shine through is by making analogies. Analogies compare two things, to either clarify or explain. Comedians often use analogies in their routines to make us laugh and give us a new perspective.

Here are a few examples:

- "The culture at my company is like *Game of Thrones*. I want to work somewhere where the vibe is *Modern Family*."

- "Explaining a joke is like dissecting a frog. You understand it better but the frog dies in the process." —André Maurois

Analogies are a fun and powerful way to shed new light on things. Definitely experiment with these in your talks!

Either Avoid Clichés or Add Your Own Twist to Them

"You are what you eat."
"Actions speak louder than words."
"You can't judge a book by its cover."
Clichés will not add personal style to your presentation. These phrases are so overused that they have lost their bite and power. They no longer have the ability to make your audience sit up and take notice. So, when you are writing your talk, avoid using clichés. That said, if you can get clever with a cliché in a way that serves your message, then go for it!

I recently had a client who was working on a presentation about healthy eating. She wanted to encourage people to eat grass-fed beef instead of beef that had been fed GMO corn. I loved it and laughed when she said, "You are what *they* eat." She played with a phrase we've heard over and over again to make her point. Her new creation was memorable.

Here's a cliché I played with earlier in this chapter: "A picture is worth a thousand words." My twist on the cliché: "A picture may be worth a thousand words, but a great story is made up of a thousand pictures." (To be very clear, I do not mean that you should have a thousand slides in your presentation! Instead, paint pictures for your audience with your words.)

Using Humor Wisely

I highly recommend mixing humor into your talk when appropriate. It's a great way to connect with your audience and bring the group together. If you don't feel you are particularly funny, enlist a friend or colleague to suggest a few fun comments or anecdotes that you would feel comfortable saying.

Here are some ways you that could approach being humorous:

- Subvert your audience's expectations with misdirection. If you know what people are expecting you to say, go in a different direction. Here are two great examples of this:

    1. My friend Alex worked in a school system where the superintendent had just announced his retirement. Many people in the community were expecting Alex to move into that role. However, my friend had no intention of doing this; he was happy with what he was currently doing. Fully aware of what was on the minds of the teachers at a recent meeting, Alex said, "Thank you all for being here today. In case you were wondering, all the rumors are true. *(long pause)* I am getting my hair cut later this afternoon." (Alex then pointed to his reasonably short hair, which didn't look like it needed to be cut.) The crowd laughed. He addressed what was true—their expectation of an announcement—but then went in a totally different direction. Adding to the fun, when he later saw some of the teachers at another event, they complimented him on his new haircut.

    2. My client, a funny guy who is also an actor, brought in some humor when he officiated his friends' wedding. Scott said, "Dearly beloved, we are gathered here today to bear witness and celebrate an extremely important milestone, one year in

the making: my debut as a wedding officiant." He set up the expectation that he would talk about the bride and groom, but then talked about himself.

- Consider using a funny analogy or edited cliché.
- Always use your judgment in terms of humor. If you are making a joke in regard to someone on your team or in your group, be kind and don't embarrass them. (If you are invited to participate in what's known as a roast, that's different.) If you are wondering if your humor is too edgy or in poor taste, run it by someone you trust who understands the context. Tread very, very carefully when it comes to making jokes about politics, current events, and hot-button topics. You don't want people to leave your talk focused on your ill-chosen humor rather than your important content.

Endings

Great stories, hilarious jokes, and powerful presentations all have strong endings. Often the ending is a statement that ties everything together. It's also a place where your personality and style can shine through and leave the readers on a positive note. You also want it to be abundantly clear that you have finished.

Imagine that I am wrapping up my presentation on the topic of managing your nerves. Among other things, I've talked about accepting and being present with your feelings rather than judging them. I've shared that it is better to have passion and energy than to be totally calm. Here's a possible ending: "The next time you are tempted to freak out about butterflies, I want you to picture their tiny, delicate feet breakdancing in your stomach. Even if they do a number from *Thriller*, they are just not that threatening, right?"

My goals with this ending are to give my audience a new and comedic way to think about butterflies and a practical tip to try—and I want them to smile.

Be Sure to Avoid Jargon

For your story to fully make sense to your audience, you may need to provide context or background information. If you are speaking within your organization, there may be references, acronyms, product names, jargon, or clients that everyone knows. But if you are talking to someone who is not from your company, without providing context, your story will probably not make sense.

You may need to contextualize when things happened, or what certain terms, job titles, or acronyms mean. Imagine that I am speaking to an audience who knows nothing about me, and I say:

"Hi, everyone! When you are at a crossroads, it's important to get the support you need so you can make the best decisions. When I worked for BRB, I had the role of HID. But I started to get bored and wondered if their SMART vision really aligned with my goals. Then I spoke to Leonardo, who gave me some great guidance."

Here are all the things that would be confusing for someone in the audience who did not know me or my company:

- What type of crossroads am I referring to?
- What is BRB? What do they do?
- What does HID stand for?

- What is a SMART vision?
- Who the heck is Leonardo?
- And who am I?

Here's a new version of the same speech where I have added context, so that people can follow my story better.

"Hi, everyone! I'm Kim and I'm a life coach. I provide guidance to people so they can live their lives with intention and purpose. When you are at a crossroads, making an important life decision, it's especially important to get the support you need so you can make the best choices. When I worked for Best Reliable Banking, or BRB, I had the role of HID, Head of Inspirational Development. But I started to get bored. BRB had something called a SMART vision. SMART stood for Successful Managers Are Really Thriving. I was a manager, but sadly, I wasn't thriving anymore. I hadn't been for two years. Then I spoke to Leonardo, my life coach, who gave me some great guidance about following my own path."

In the second example I've clarified all of the abbreviations and lingo and explained who people are. My story is much less confusing now that the listener has context. When you are working on your talk, be on the lookout for words, jargon, or names that your audience may not know so you can be sure to clarify them. You don't want them to look at you blankly.

Humanize Facts and Figures When Possible

If you are sharing data during your presentation, you can empower your numbers to make a stronger impact by giving them a more recognizable context and by humanizing them. In other words, add more information so that your audience considers not only numbers but also people.

Here's an example. The US Department of Health and Human Services reports that 116 people a day die from opioid-related drug overdoses. This is already a shocking number, but what if we look at it from an even broader perspective? For example:

"In the US, 116 people a day die from opioid-related drug overdoses. That is a heartbreaking number. In Massachusetts, a whopping 86.4 percent of people twelve and older who suffer from drug abuse or dependence go untreated.

"These numbers are highly disturbing. But let's not forget that addicts are not the only ones affected by addiction. Think of their loved ones, partners, and children. Think of their friends, coworkers, and bosses. The number of people affected by addiction is actually much higher."

In this example I gave the numbers more perspective to help the audience see the problem in a new light. This will create a sense of urgency that can spur people to take action.

Lists

If you think of yourself as a guide for your audience, there are things you can do to make it easier for them to follow you. Say you have five points you would like to make on a particular subject. Let your audience know there will be five points you are going to cover. They will then follow along with you more closely, waiting to find out what the next one is. Here is an example:

"From the folks at ReachOut.com, here are five steps to help you study better.

"Number one: Don't be too afraid of stress. Not all stress is bad; some stress is a good motivator. Just be aware if it switches from being motivating to becoming overwhelming.

"Number two: Study in twenty-minute increments—this is the most effective use of your brain power.

"Number three: A great way to learn and remember is to say what you're learning out loud without any notes.

"Number four: Planned and timed breaks are great, but jumping on your phone every five minutes will really break your concentration.

"Number five: You will remember more of what you studied if you get a good night's sleep, rather than cramming all night long."

Making Great Slides

Here's the thing: you are the main event, and your slides are your witty sidekick. Some people have this concept backward. They put all of their prep time into creating their slides. Then, when in front of their audience, they put all of their focus on their slides and basically read them to their captive guests. This may feel like a safe choice, because it allows the presenter to hide and avoid the audience. But it is not a wise or powerful strategy. You might as well send everyone an email.

Ideally, your slides should do what you cannot. Your slides can:

- Reveal compelling images that help explain your ideas
- Show a relevant and fascinating video clip
- Share an important graph or chart
- Break down complex concepts
- Support the humor in your talk

Author and speaker Jia Jiang gave a TED Talk about how he spent one hundred days seeking rejection. His talk is really funny, engaging, and powerful. He did a great job having his slides be his witty sidekick. At one point Jiang mentioned a letter he wrote to his family as a child, describing his dream to eventually run a company so powerful that it would buy Microsoft.

In his next slide he revealed the letter—and it was almost entirely in Chinese. This meant that many people in his audience could not read it. Jiang commented, "I did highlight some key words." These were the only English words and there were only three of them scattered throughout the page: Basic, Windows, and Microsoft. The fact that many in the audience could not decipher the letter was really funny. What is not funny is when you have slides that are covered head to toe in words, even if they are in a language the audience understands.

Words

When I see a slide that is covered in text, I find it visually overwhelming. I pay less attention to the speaker and I jump ahead, trying to read all of the points on the slide. Sometimes I give up entirely and tune out. White space is your friend. When slides have fewer words on them, it is easier for your audience to focus on what is there.

How Many Slides Should I Use?

When preparing your slide deck, see how few slides you can have. This does *not* mean you should cram as much as you can into fewer slides. Challenge yourself to be creative with your slides' images and text. When rehearsing, as you go through each one, ask yourself, "Why does this slide matter?" If you can't justify it, cut it.

No matter what time of day you are presenting, your audience will appreciate fewer words:

- If you are the first speaker of the day, your audience may still be only starting to feel the effects of their tall, nonfat latte with caramel drizzle. Overwhelming them with data is a real turnoff and you may lose them.
- If you are speaking right after lunch, your audience's pasta tiredness may start to kick in. Boring slides will only make your audience want to nap more.
- If you have the last slot of the day, you can imagine how potentially overloaded your audience's brains will be. All the more reason to stay present in each moment with each new bit of information you share verbally and on your slides.

There are some circumstances when you are limited as to the number of slides you can present. (Whoever decided that you can have only X slides probably has experienced "death by PowerPoint" in the past and decided, "Never again!") This is good news, for it will force you to include only what is essential. Even if you *think* you are being conservative with what is on your slides, there may still be quite a bit on there. To avoid overwhelming your audience, reveal one graphic or one bullet point of text at a time on each individual slide. This will keep you and your audience present, in the moment.

Consider using a font that captures the mood of what you are trying to express—there are so many options to choose from! But don't go crazy using something that is difficult to read. Using bold, italics, and underline can help your main points, titles, or subtitles to stand out, as can color choices and using all caps. You could also consider a handout or follow-up email on topics that you want them to digest in order to minimize what you're putting on slides.

Graphics

A great image can evoke emotion, interest, empathy, questions, and laughter. If you or your organization has photos that tell a compelling story, use them! These will be much more powerful than bullet points with text. If you don't have images that serve you, check out some of the amazing resources available online. Some sites offer royalty-free images (to use them, you simply give the photographer credit), and some require you to pay.

Spending time finding visuals that make your slides come to life is worth it. I recently saw slides that contained pictures of innovative hospital spaces for smiling expectant moms in Africa that I will never forget. A few months ago I viewed a presentation that included stark and sobering images from a recent protest that portrayed both despair and hopefulness in a way that words could not. These were great examples of slides doing what the speaker could not. You can also use images to communicate symbolically.

Graphs and Charts

It is often necessary to include graphs and/or charts in scientific and business presentations. The easier these are to read, the better. Be sure to see how these graphics look when they are projected on a larger screen to determine if they are clear enough or if you need to increase their quality. You may need to enlarge the text or change the colors you are using. If you are stuck with an image that does not look great but is all you have, it will be up to you to help your audience understand it.

Say you have a difficult-to-read graph that has many small numbers, colors, and wavy lines. You could say, "I know this graph is hard to read, but let me show you what's important to take away from this image. If you look here [use laser pointer to indicate the area you are mentioning], you'll see the frequency is X. Now look here [use laser pointer to indicate the new area you are mentioning], you'll see the frequency has increased to Y. This was not an expected result. It led us to wonder if…"

Proper Use of Laser Pointers

In regard to laser pointers, use them sparingly. They can really help your audience to navigate slides with complex images, such as X-rays or crowded graphs, but they can also be super annoying. It is important to never shine a laser pointer in your own or anyone else's eyes, because the beam can cause retinal damage. Also, do not shine it into a mirror or other reflecting surfaces. Use your judgment, rehearse with the laser pointer in advance, and use it only when you need to.

Interacting with Your Witty Sidekick

You've decided that you are not going to face your slides and read them word for word to an annoyed audience. Good! This means you will be facing your audience. If you are holding a clicker that advances your slides, keep it in the hand that enables you to keep your body open to the audience.

Here's an example of how to do this when you are moving around the stage: imagine that you are in a room that is very wide and has a wide screen that takes up much of the wall. Your laptop is in the center, close to the screen. You have decided to stand to the right side of the screen for some of your talk and the left side for other parts of your talk. You are choosing to do this so that:

1. You will not be blocking the screen.
2. You can engage equally with both sides of your audience.

If you begin your talk standing to the right of the screen (stage right), hold the clicker in your left hand. When you to move to the left side of the screen (stage left), hold the clicker in your right hand. Not only will these choices keep you open to your audience physically, but they will also help you to be heard better if you are not using a microphone. If you are holding the clicker in your right hand when you are on the right side of the screen, you will need to twist your body toward the laptop to advance the slide. If you are then spending time explaining a complex chart while facing the screen, you may not be heard as well because you are facing away from the audience.

If it makes the most sense to stand in the same spot for the whole presentation, just be sure to hold the clicker in the hand that will keep you open to the audience.

Timing Is Everything

You may have a temptation to rush when you are going through your slides. Perhaps you fear that you have too many, or you just want to get the presentation over with. You would not be alone. Many people rush, but it does not serve them and it will not serve you or your audience. When you are speaking about a slide, stay engaged with your audience until you are completely finished. Only then should you advance to the next slide.

When clients are practicing in front of me, I will witness something like this: (Presenter is facing audience.)

"In this slide you can see that our sales increased in July and August of this year." (Presenter knows that he is near the end of this slide's content. His mind is already moving on to the next slide, though he is about to say important information about the current slide. He is looking at his notes, and his voice starts to trail off.) "This is 40 percent above last year's summer sales."

His last line is good news! But he is not present, nor is he enjoying sharing this great information.

Take two: (Presenter is facing audience.)

"In this slide you can see that our sales increased in July and August of this year." (Presenter knows that he is about to share some good news, so he is completely present, still engaged with the audience. He enjoys sharing his next line and emphasizes "40 percent above.") "This is 40 percent above last year's summer sales." (Audience is impressed.)

When you advance to your next slide, bring in more energy. I tell my clients, "Treat your new slide like it is a brand-new day." This will help your audience to keep engaged and follow you on the journey.

You may have slides that contain valuable information, but you don't necessarily need to spend your time speaking extensively about all of it in detail. Here's an example: your last slide lists resources that the audience could look into on their own. You could say, "My final slide includes a list of government agencies that you can reach out to if your department needs any additional information. I will leave the slide up during the Q&A. Feel free to take a picture of the slide so you will have the correct contact information."

When Technology Is Not Your Friend

Technology can be fickle. It can amaze you and then leave you in despair within the same five minutes. I want you to think positively about your future presentations, but I also want you to be prepared for whatever life throws your way. Take some time to contemplate what you will do if you are unable to use your laptop or get your slides to work. Could you bring hard copies of the presentation? Can you make sure the final version of your talk is saved to the cloud so that you can access it from anywhere? Can you share your message without your slides? Do you have a backup laptop available? Do you know who to reach out to for tech support if anything goes wrong? Expect the best, but prepare for misbehaving technology.

Rehearsal

Now it's time to rehearse! When people prepare for a presentation or toast, they tend to invest a lot of time creating the slide deck or speech and less time actually saying their words out loud. They may run over it in their heads, but this is not the same as a live rehearsal. Live rehearsal is a crucial part of the preparation process. It is a great opportunity to troubleshoot. You can see if there are awkward transitions or words that are difficult to pronounce, or if the shoes you chose are a bad idea.

The Power of Rehearsals

As Mark Twain said, "It usually takes me more than three weeks to prepare a good impromptu speech." As you rehearse, new ideas and insights might even come to you along the way. Not only will you get increasingly comfortable with your material and slides or notes, but you may also connect your dots in a new, more compelling way.

This is the time for you to tie together all the components of a good presentation. Your rehearsal ideally should help you:

- Make sure that your script, notes, or outline will serve you well.
- Get really familiar with the content so you can be present with your audience moment to moment and not distracted by trying to remember what to say.
- Practice with your technology (if it is part of your presentation) so you can coordinate your words and images to make the biggest impact possible.

- Be intentional and strategic with your body language and movement to command the room.
- Be creative with your vocal variety to engage, entice, surprise, and motivate your audience.

You can rehearse on your own and then invite some trusted colleagues, friends, or loved ones to be your test audience. (To learn how to best manage this experience, see the section "Soliciting Feedback from Friends, Family, and/or Colleagues" later in this chapter.) By inviting a few friendly folks to be in your audience while you rehearse, you will be gradually increasing the outside stimuli that you are encountering. A client of mine who was preparing for a TED Talk got in front of many different groups, large and small, in a variety of settings to rehearse. She wanted to challenge herself to handle many different situations and rooms.

Finding Outside Help

A public speaking coach can also be helpful for the rehearsal process. Many of my clients have practiced their talk in front of me because of my expertise but also because I am completely separate from their work and social life. *Google* can help you to see what your options are. If you've found a few coaches who interest you, chat with each one briefly to see how they work with clients to help you determine who will be the best fit for you.

What to Rehearse

If it is at all possible, visit the room where you will be presenting to rehearse. Walk around the space to get familiar with it and practice your delivery. See if you can try out the technology.

In addition to rehearsing your talk or toast, rehearse some logistical things as well, such as:

- Your introduction, your hand gestures, and movement.
- Your technology, use of the microphone, and your notes.
- Taking sips of water. (I have spent time strategizing the best place for a client to put his water bottle so that it could in no way accidentally spill on his laptop.)
- Walking from your chair (or the back of the room) to the front of the room where you will be speaking.

The following activity will guide you to make the most of this action during your rehearsal process.

Activity: Practice Getting Up to the Front

If possible, do this activity in a room that has some space to move in. If you do not have an upcoming public speaking event that you are preparing for, imagine one that you may encounter in the future.

1. Sit in a chair that is facing the rest of the room. Imagine that the stage is on the other side of the room. Sit BIG, OPEN, and DIRECT (refer back to the "Exploring Body Language Choices" activity in Chapter 3). Sink into the chair, really feeling your feet on the floor and your body in the seat. Take several belly breaths.
2. Choose an encouraging statement to say to yourself, like "I got this!" or "I'm excited to share what I know!" while you are still seated.
3. Imagine the host introduces you. Walk with your head held high to the front of the room.

4. Once you get to the front, turn around to face the rest of the room, with your feet firmly planted about hip-distance apart. Don't lock your knees.

5. Smile at your imaginary audience. Envision yourself as their host. Take a few deep breaths.

6. Choose an empowering objective, such as "I am here to shine light on an important problem that needs to be addressed," "I am here to help my audience learn something new," or "I am here to inspire my audience to be kinder to themselves." Say it to yourself and out loud.

7. Remind yourself that this experience is not about you. It is about giving to the audience.

8. Greet your audience. If you are in the midst of preparing for a specific talk or toast, then go right into it. Feel free to repeat these steps a number of times so that you are creating a new habit.

Real-World Example:
Andrew Builds a Rehearsal Process

Here is an example of a client, a TV chef, who created a new rehearsal process that enabled him to be in the moment and have more fun while filming. Andrew is a chef on a cooking show who travels around the country and explores different unique eating spots. In each place he connects with the folks who create amazing dishes, samples their wares, and gets the scoop on what's special about the cooking process, or the quirky background of a tasty dish. Once he's back home, he invests time and energy recreating the dish with his team. Then it's showtime!

During an episode Andrew will chat with the host about his experience at a particular eatery and then demonstrate how to cook their special dish. Not only is it necessary for him to have all of the details of the recipe memorized, but he also needs to banter with the host while keeping on track with the required steps.

When we first met, Andrew wanted to have more fun with storytelling, and to feel less nervous both preparing for the shoot and while on set. One of his challenges was that he filmed episodes only twice a year, so it was difficult to create an empowering preparation routine.

To connect him to his passion, joy, and personality, I asked Andrew what he loved about food and his job. As he described his love of cooking and delicious food, and his quirky experiences on the road, I could see him relax and become more playful. I wanted to help him bring these aspects of himself front and center while on set. Though his official title for the show was not "host," I did encourage Andrew to think of himself as a host in his own kitchen. I wanted him to operate from a place of generosity and sharing, rather than being under pressure to be perfect, second-guessing himself, and having no fun.

Ideally, Andrew's job was to help the audience feel like they were right there in the kitchen, cooking with him. He needed to bring to life the unique characters he met, the interesting places he visited, and the things he learned. Andrew was the audience's nose, taste buds, and cooking guide.

My goal was to bring lightness and humor to the brainstorming and rehearsal process. Not only would a sense of ease and play help Andrew with any nerves, but it would also make the show more fun. I encouraged him to paint a vivid picture with his words. Did he get up crazy early in the freezing cold? Did he and his fellow crew member drive down a winding country road with no signs? What did it smell like when he entered the space? What was the decor like?

During this process, Andrew fleshed out what was unusual and distinct about his experience and the star of the show, the food. Once filming, Andrew wouldn't have time to share the entire story with all of its details, but our process helped him to choose the juiciest and most relevant aspects for the shoot days.

Another important step was to make his script user-friendly. The original document was overwhelming, with many long sentences written in a small font. His revised script was much easier on the eyes—ideas, rather than sentences, were listed with bullet points. The script was typed in a larger font, and there was much more white space. The use of bullet points also took the pressure off of him feeling obligated to say exactly the same wording during every take.

When it was time to rehearse, I played host. Because the show is instructional, it was important that there be lessons along the way about Andrew's choice of ingredients or cooking techniques. As we rehearsed, we talked through any complicated steps or topics so that he could simplify them for himself and, ultimately, his audience. I bantered with Andrew, and he practiced responding in the moment to whatever I threw his way. Going through the recipe for accuracy was the goal for some run-throughs. Other run-throughs were focused on being playful with his story and spontaneous banter. As the shoot dates got closer, Andrew integrated all of the elements.

The more Andrew could trust that he deeply knew the ingredients, their measurements, and the recipe's step-by-step process, the freer he was to enjoy each moment. He had more bandwidth to interact with me and still keep the recipe on track.

I reminded Andrew that even though the camera would be on him, the shoot was not about him. He was there to invite the viewers into his world, to share what he had learned, and to be hospitable. He was there to teach the audience the best way to make a new, yummy dish. And lucky him—he was also there to sample the food at the end of the episode.

Over time Andrew became increasingly comfortable and confident. He now has much more fun preparing for shoots and being on set because he has a rehearsal process he can count on. His efforts have paid off: he's received great feedback from the director, producers, and colleagues on the show! (And I've gotten to eat some yummy treats!)

To Memorize or Not to Memorize

To memorize or not memorize, that is the question.
Whether 'tis wiser to know every single word
Or to have bullet points guide you along the way.

Actors and presenters have many similar traits. They both need to know what they are saying and why. Some actors write their own material, just as many speakers create their own presentations and pitches. Actors sometimes get hired to do staged readings where they are able to rely on a script, but they are still doing their best to deliver the lines in a conversational and real way. There are occasions when you will be using a "script" of some sort. You may be delivering a maid-of-honor or best-man speech, officiating a wedding, delivering a keynote at a conference, or serving as a graduation speaker. In these circumstances your job will be to bring the words on the page to life so they seem spontaneous and are conversational.

In the situations when it is not appropriate for you to hold an actual script while presenting, the question of memorization comes up. Should you treat your presentation like lines in a script and memorize every single word? Should you set in stone exactly *how* you are going to say every word and phrase?

As for memorizing every word, this is an important and helpful goal for many. But for some people, this feels too restrictive. Also, there are some circumstances when word for word memorization is not the best choice, as in the example of Andrew the TV chef earlier in this chapter.

I'm not a fan of setting in stone exactly how you are going to say every word and phrase. This approach may make you feel like you are more in control of the talk, but to the audience it will sound like you are not fully present, that you are on autopilot.

How to Memorize

Here are some memorization strategies for when you are working with a full script:

- **Type out your words in a big, easy-to-read font.** Break down paragraphs into smaller sections. Create a script that is easy on the eyes, with a lot of white space.
- **Read your talk from beginning to end, slowly and out loud, several times.** You will start to become familiar with the order. Images will also probably come to mind. Reading out loud will enable you to hear it as well as visualize it. You may stumble over awkward wording that reads better in your script than it does when it is said out loud. What works on the page doesn't always work on the stage! You may discover sections that need to be clarified. Good! Better to become aware of these now and fix them as you rehearse.

- **Make sure you understand *why* you are saying each sentence.** When you get clear on your objective, things will flow more naturally.

- **Plan your movement.** If you will be moving around on the stage, if possible, determine what your movement will be while learning your script. That way, you can identify that when you move right, you say "X," and when you move left you say "Y."

- **Use alliteration to help you remember sentences.** Identify alliteration—any places where you see multiple words with the same first letter, as in this sentence: "My llama Lucy loves to socialize with the other llamas, Lyle and Lloyd." There are a lot of "L" words here. It may help you to remember that there are three "L" words at the beginning of the sentence and three at the end.

- **Write down your script from memory.** See how you do. Try again. As you do this, connect your words to your objectives. Remembering *why* you say the lines will help you to remember their content and order.

- **Record yourself.** If you are an auditory learner (meaning that you learn well through listening), you can record yourself saying your pitch or script slowly and then listen to it repeatedly. I highly recommend that when you record it you say it without a lot of vocal variety. Keep it really simple so that you can focus on learning what the words are rather than how to say them. Once you start getting them down, you can play with varying your vocal choices.

- **Play with extremes with pacing.** Deliver one paragraph very, very fast. Then do the next one very slowly, and so on. This is not the way you will ultimately deliver your talk; it will simply stretch the range of options you have to choose from. You can also play with dramatic pauses, pitch, and volume in this extreme way.

Owning Your Lines

One of the biggest challenges for presenters and actors is to memorize their lines and then, when onstage or on set, make it sound as though their ideas are newly unfolding. The challenge is that when they get really attached to how they say each word, this can lead to the words seeming overly rehearsed, unnatural, mechanical, and not very engaging. In this circumstance, the performer has predetermined exactly how they want to deliver each line and left no room for inspiration to strike in the moment.

The ideal circumstance is that you will have rehearsed enough so that you know *what* you will be saying, but you have not determined how every word, phrase, and sentence will be delivered. Instead, you have explored choices when rehearsing and incorporated lots of variety but allowed room for spontaneity. Then, when you present, you are present in the moment rather than on autopilot.

Helpful Stage Terminology That Actors and Directors Use

When you determine where and when you are going to move around onstage, this is called blocking. When you have the whole talk memorized and no longer need your script, this is called being "off book." "Stage right" refers to the right side of the stage from the performer's perspective (when they are looking out at the audience). "Stage left" refers to the left side of the stage from the performer's perspective.

Real-World Example:
Jennifer Is on a Tight Deadline and Wonders
How to Best Memorize Her Talk

Three days before she was scheduled to present, Jennifer and I met for the first time. Her conference talk was written and her slides were ready. She was allotted eighteen minutes for her presentation, but it was running a bit long. Jennifer felt pressured to speak quickly so she could fit everything in. She was very familiar with the story she wanted to tell but had not yet memorized it. In the past, when she worked with bullet points instead of a full script, she would ramble, which, given the time limit, she couldn't afford to do. Sticking to her script helped her be concise, but holding it and reading it word for word wasn't an option.

I suggested a preparation strategy that included a combination of shortening the talk, creating bullets, and memorization. First, we went through the script together to determine what could be cut. Not only would this take the pressure off time-wise, but it would also make the speech tighter and better. We also reviewed her goals for each section. Once Jennifer got really clear on her objectives and the picture she was painting for each, remembering the flow would become easier. She then rehearsed on her own, creating bullets and also memorizing certain sections.

The day before her presentation Jennifer had a tech rehearsal. Her deck consisted of a few slides containing powerful images and a small amount of text. At the rehearsal she found out that there was a large screen at the base of the stage that would be visible only to her. She then created her note slides, including direct quotes and points she wanted to be sure to share, as well as thumbnails of the slides the audience would see. Her words were written in a large, bold, colorful font so that they were easy to read. The tech folks synched up her note slides with the presentation slides her audience would be seeing. During her rehearsal she figured out how to discreetly look at her notes while still engaging with the audience. This whole process enabled her to be ready to successfully give her talk and enjoy the ride.

Working with Notes

Some people prefer to work from a script; others prefer to work with an outline or bullets. Whichever your preference, make them easy to read and number the pages so that if you accidentally drop them, it will be easy to get them back in the correct order. Some presenters choose to put their script in a binder, to keep it all together. If you are reading from a script, hold up the script so that you can see your audience and still easily glance at your script. (If you hold it too low, you will tend to look down.) The more familiar you are with your script, the easier it will be to make eye contact with your audience from time to time (the more you can do this, the better!). If your script includes important information, such as "turn to the bride and groom" or "go to slide four," put these directions in a different color or font size so they are really easy to see. Rehearse using your notes or script so you can troubleshoot. If you will be using a microphone, find out if it is a handheld mic. If so, you will need to figure out how to best hold your script and the mic.

Soliciting Feedback from Friends, Family, and/or Colleagues

Have you ever asked a friend or family member to give you feedback on a project and then, when they did, you regretted asking them? Perhaps their criticism felt too harsh or was not well articulated. Maybe they said, "I don't know. I just didn't get what you were trying to say." Or did you wonder if some tension from another interaction, having nothing to do with the task at hand, was clouding things? Getting *constructive* feedback is invaluable. The opposite? Not so much.

Receiving insightful feedback can make an incredible difference. Here are some steps that will help you to set yourself up for success when asking for input:

1. Choose your test audience wisely. Be thoughtful about who you ask.

   - Do you trust that they really have your best interest at heart?
   - Do they know about your subject matter? If not, does it matter?
   - Do they have time to give you their undivided attention? Or are they so overwhelmed with their own work and life that even if they want to help you, they will be distracted?

2. Manage expectations—both for you and your "audience members." Before you run through your presentation, set clear guidelines. Your parameters will shape how your audience members take in what you are sharing:

- Tell your audience what kind of feedback would be helpful to you. For example, if you are early in your preparation process and you simply want feedback on your rough ideas, let them know that. If you are getting close to the day you are presenting and you want to know what you could cut from the presentation to save time, tell them.
- Let them know any other details you may want them to keep in mind as they settle in to listen, watch, and take notes, such as:

Vocally:
- Am I rushing or going too slow?
- Can you understand everything I am saying?
- Do I use a lot of filler words, like *um*, *you know*, and *like*?

Body language:
- Do I look confident?
- Am I doing anything distracting with my hands?
- Am I moving too much or too little?

Storytelling:
- Do my stories and examples keep your interest?
- When do you lose interest?
- Do my transitions between topics make sense?
- Am I getting too bogged down in details at some points?
- Do my beginning and ending pack a punch?

Slides:
- Are the graphs and charts in my slides correct?
- Are my slides too busy?
- Are the transitions between slides working?

Gratitude:
- Have I remembered to mention everyone who contributed?
- Is there anyone else who needs to be thanked?

If you have a variety of folks watching, you could assign them different aspects to focus on. For example, when I attend rehearsals of scientific presentations, my job is to be aware of many elements of the talk, but scientists well versed in the subject matter are typically there to make sure the science is accurately conveyed verbally and on slides.

After the run-through steer the conversation toward the topics you asked people to be aware of. Once that is covered, open it up to a general discussion. Take notes on the feedback and/or record it on your phone (after you ask permission to do so from everyone). It's understandable that you may be tired and fried in the days leading up to your talk, so don't put pressure on yourself to remember everything. You could also ask someone else to take notes. As you mull over the feedback you received, consider all that you learned, but don't feel pressured to incorporate every single suggestion. Use your judgment.

Real-World Example:
Kate Prepares for a Video Promoting Her New Book

Kate Perry is rated "New York's Best Dog Trainer" by *New York* magazine. She needed help preparing for a video shoot. The video's ultimate purpose would be to help launch her book, *Training for Both Ends of the Leash.*

As you can imagine, Kate has a tremendous amount of knowledge about dogs and how to best train them. She could potentially talk for hours on the subject. Our goal was to find the most important elements of her book to highlight for the video. We ultimately wanted viewers to get a sense of what was unique and different about Kate's approach to training. It was important that she concisely articulate her philosophy and methods while still allowing her warmth and friendliness to shine through.

We discussed who would be potentially watching the video and why. Then we brainstormed and crafted her talking points. Her goal was for current and future dog owners to know that her book was a go-to guide whether they were housetraining their first puppy or trying to teach an old dog new ways to play in the park. Kate wrote her talking points on separate index cards in big print. This helped familiarize her with her ideas and memorize wording that she really liked. Kate could experiment with the order of her ideas by simply rearranging her index cards.

Of course, we wanted Kate to look her best, so we discussed what clothing would work well on camera. As a dog trainer, she dresses casually, so that was the look she wanted for the shoot. Solid colors work well for filming, so she found a simple, light blue V-neck shirt and some nice jeans. Most importantly, Kate felt really comfortable in her outfit. She also booked a hair appointment with a trusted hairdresser that helped her to feel camera-ready.

By the time she was on set, Kate felt prepared and ready to go. She knew what she wanted to say and focused on being an upbeat and caring trainer, excited to share her wisdom.

Activity: Draft a Short Talk, Rehearse, and Share It

This activity will guide you through creating a short talk, rehearsing it, and presenting it. You can present it to a room full of furniture, a motley crew of stuffed animals, or some friends, family, coworkers, or a takeout delivery guy. It's up to you. Choosing a subject that you genuinely care about will make this exercise more powerful and fun. Take note of any negative beliefs that cross your mind during the following steps. You don't have to buy into any of these thoughts. Take a breath, then let those thoughts float away. Grab a notepad or your laptop.

1. Choose a problem that you are passionate about. Jot down why it matters to you and needs to matter to others.
2. Decide what audience would benefit from learning about this problem and your solution(s). (Examples: dog owners, international students, entrepreneurs, teenagers struggling with eating disorders.)
3. Determine what location would be ideal for this kind of talk. (Examples: a high school auditorium, your conference room at work, a Boys & Girls Club, a conference devoted to addressing environmental issues.)

Now that you have figured out your "what" (what you are going to talk about), your "who" (who you are going to be sharing with), your "why" (why your topic matters), and your "where" (the ideal location for giving your talk), it's time to work on your "how" (how you will use language to engage your audience, paint a picture of the problem, offer your solution(s), and inspire them to action).

The following are structural elements to guide you:

1. Include a short story with details to help the audience understand the problem and/or solution.
2. Include three strategies that will help solve this problem.
3. Have a really compelling opening sentence.
4. At some point introduce yourself.
5. Include a call to action.

Here are the steps to follow:

1. Brainstorm. Let yourself be messy with your process, and see what your imagination and memory bring to you. Once you feel you have some ideas, start to put them into some kind of order that flows. Play around with this until it feels like it flows smoothly.
2. Create notes that work for you. You could write an outline or have a list of bullet points. You could stop there or you could write out your talk in full sentences.

Now it's time to rehearse your talk. Ground yourself by connecting to your "why." Why is it important that your audience learn from you? What is in it for them? Again, your audience can be stuffed animals or the pictures hanging on the walls.

Experiment with vocal variety—modulate your pitch, pace, and volume, and include pauses. Be intentional about how you carry yourself, experiment with BIG, OPEN, DIRECT, and BRIGHT or BUBBLY or SOFT in different combinations If you are going to move, move during transitional sentences, not when you are making major points. Now consider these final points:

1. New ideas may come to you as you rehearse. Add them to your notes and keep rehearsing.
2. Once you feel you have rehearsed enough, see if your outline, bulleted list, or full script is easy to read. If not, make tweaks so that it is easy to use.
3. Showtime! Remind yourself again why your talk is important. Share your talk with your audience! You could film yourself and watch it afterward with kindness. If you do have people watching,

you could solicit their feedback. (Review the section "Soliciting Feedback from Friends, Family, and/or Colleagues," located earlier in this chapter, to learn to do this artfully.)

4. Congrats! You did it. Review what felt great and what still needs some additional attention.

CHAPTER 6

Preparing

It's getting close to game day. Now it's time to strategize how to best maintain your focus and energy in the days leading up to your talk, event, or meeting. Having a game plan for different types of public speaking situations will also help you to take charge of your experience and avoid feeling overwhelmed.

This chapter will address what's in your control and how to cultivate an upbeat attitude toward what is not in your control. You'll learn how positive visualization can help you, as well as how to pace yourself so that your batteries are not depleted when it's time to engage with your audience and give it your all. I'll cover the ins and outs of sharing your message on camera, via Zoom or Skype, and on a webinar or podcast. Need to make a wedding toast? You'll learn some valuable tips on brainstorming, outlines, and drafts. Panels, Q&As, and introducing yourself will also be addressed, as well as a more improvisational public speaking experience—networking.

Planning

When you are planning an experience, whether it is a surprise party or a presentation to your department, your job becomes easier when you understand your audience, acknowledge what's in your control (and not), and know what you are going to wear. Having clarity on these elements will help things come together and prepare you for any curve balls that are thrown your way.

What Is in Your Control; What Is Out of Your Control

Each day we juggle the various elements of our lives; some we can control, and others we cannot. When we try to control the aspects of life that are really out of our control, we drive ourselves, and probably others, nuts. The same is true with public speaking. There are elements that you need to take charge of and others that you need to accept as being out of your hands.

For the most part, you can control:

- Your attitude—you can shift it if it becomes negative
- Your beliefs—you can let go of the ones that no longer serve you
- Your planning process—you can use your time wisely or you can procrastinate
- Your writing process
- Whether or not you ask for help
- The creation of your slide deck (unless you will be presenting one created for you)
- Your rehearsal—how much or how little

- Your physical and verbal habits (pacing too much, using filler words)
- Visiting the room that you are presenting in before you present
- Who you ask for feedback during the writing and rehearsal processes
- Your clothing choice
- Your plan if things go wrong with technological components
- Whether you have eaten enough and had enough water
- Whether you plan to go to bed early the night before
- How you respond to feedback after you present

You cannot control:

- What your audience thinks about you; you will do all you can to engage them, but ultimately you have no control over their thoughts
- The technology (beyond practicing and familiarizing yourself with how it works)
- Unplanned interruptions, like a fire drill
- The weather
- Last-minute schedule and room changes

Sometimes you can control the following, but often you cannot:

- The time of day of your presentation
- The location of your presentation
- The temperature in the room
- The marketing for your presentation
- How much sleep you get

If you are under stress, see if what is making you anxious falls under the category of things you can control. If you can control it, take charge! If you cannot, choose a belief system that will help you deal with anything that arises. It can be helpful to expect the unexpected. This doesn't mean that you should panic about all the things that could go wrong; instead, decide to take it all in stride. Having a BIG, OPEN, and LOOSE attitude will help you to creatively problem solve when you need to. I'm talking about these types of surprises:

SURPRISE	INSTEAD OF SAYING	SAY (AND THINK)
"I'm sorry, A.J., but we've had to shift your presentation from the afternoon slot to the morning slot. Sorry we're telling you this the night before."	"Oh no! I'm screwed!"	"Okay!" (I've already prepared, so a few hours' difference isn't going to make or break me—plus, my audience will be eager to start their day rather than being in a post-lunch daze.)
"Sorry, Heather, but because the morning session went over time, we're going to need you to speak for fifteen minutes less."	"&^%*#*!"	"Cool!" (I have already prioritized what parts of my message are most important to my audience, so I can zero in on those.)
"We're sorry, Anthony, but the projector is not working and our IT person is on vacation."	"I'll never be able to make this work!"	"No problem!" (The content I put on the slides is part of my speech anyway, and I can always switch to a handout format.)

The key to grace under pressure is to go with the flow. The potential negative reactions in the table will only lead to panic, pain, stress, and feeling like a victim. These are not feelings or thoughts that will help you creatively brainstorm on how to approach the new circumstances that have been thrown at you.

You are going to be much better served by keeping a cool head and not getting caught up in a side drama about how "nothing ever works out for you" or "it just isn't fair." Take a deep breath, keep going, and trust that you'll handle it. You've got this!

The Power of Visualization

Whether you have learned about visualization or not, I'm going to guess that it is something you do, consciously or unconsciously. Have you ever pictured all of the moments that could go wrong on a date or while presenting? If you are envisioning spilling wine all over yourself, saying awkward things, or blanking in front of your audience, you are visualizing in a negative way. And probably freaking yourself out.

Positive visualization, on the other hand, is visualizing positive outcomes. This is a much better use of your time and imagination. Professional athletes use this strategy to improve their performance, as do many other people in all different industries to reach their goals. Do you remember when you were a child and you could picture something you wanted to create—a tree fort, finger puppets, or a lemonade stand? You pictured what you wanted to make and then moved toward that goal. Creative positive visualization involves imagining what you would like the outcome to be, with as many details as possible.

Activity: Positive Visualization

Let's walk through the steps of positive visualization:

1. Sit comfortably in a chair, on a sofa, or on your bed. I recommend doing these exercises first thing in the morning (to get your day off to a great start) or when you are going to bed (so you can excitedly and strategically contemplate your next day).

2. Paint pictures in your imagination of the outcome you are dreaming about. Include all of the sights and sounds around you and how it feels to be you. Consider your emotions, the expression on your face, and even your outfit.

3. You don't need to concern yourself with exactly how your visualization will come to pass. Let go of any controlling thoughts or feelings, such as "I have to close this particular account." Instead, picture celebrating thriving new partnerships with fascinating, inspiring people and brand-new big accounts.(When you're done visualizing, you will need to take logical and intentional steps toward making your vision a reality, but for now let go of overthinking how it will all come together.) Think back to the body language choices in Chapter 3—the experience of visualization ideally feels BIG, OPEN, and LOOSE. If you start to feel tight, that may mean that you are trying to figure everything out and fretting. Just paint those visual pictures and let go of any need to control the outcome. Move toward your vision with curiosity and detachment.

Taking Care of Yourself

The process of preparing and presenting can be time-consuming and stressful at times, so it's important to remember the importance of self-care. Every time you are faced with a new challenge, it's so helpful to get support from others and, especially, from yourself. Here are some things to consider the next time you take on a new public speaking challenge:

- When exactly will you carve out time to brainstorm, write, and practice?
- If you have a hectic schedule the week or day of your presentation, how will you pace yourself?
- Is there a way to make sure you don't skip meals during this process? Can you still creatively fit exercise into your routine? Eating enough and exercising will definitely help your process.
- If you foresee that you will have many presentations in one day, how will you manage your energy and focus?
- What will be your strategy for moving forward positively if certain things don't go as planned?

Use these prompts to be thoughtful and deliberate about taking care of your health and energy level. If possible, avoid all-nighters. Exercising is a great way to manage stress. Getting enough sleep will allow your waking hours to be more creative and productive. Just as the body needs rest after lifting weights, you, too, will need breaks during your preparation and rehearsal processes. So take them!

Real-World Example:
Sasha Prepares for a Two-Day Interview

Recently, I've worked with several clients who've had to undergo lengthy and grueling interviews for positions they were seeking. When I met Sasha, she was gearing up for a two-day interview at a local university.

Over the course of two days she would be having back-to-back interviews with various faculty in the chemistry department. There would be additional meetings over lunch and dinner. At the end of the second day, when Sasha was really tired after hours of constant conversation, she would need to summon her energy to present an engaging lecture about her own research for an hour to the general public and faculty. After this there would be a Q&A. And then another dinner.

To get ready for this marathon she practiced her research talk many times, adjusting slides, wording, tone, body language, and movement. We also created a strategy for her to manage her energy over this extremely focused, important, and intense forty-eight hours. For example, we discussed:

- The shoes Sasha would wear and what materials she would take with her while trudging all over campus for the various interviews
- Having healthy, energizing snacks—like cheese sticks and almonds—in her bag at all times
- Staying hydrated
- The best times to use the restroom
- The easiest foods to eat while meeting during meals
- How much caffeine would be helpful
- What to do if it was raining outside

- How she could incorporate running into her schedule leading up to the interview to help manage any stress that came up
- How to recover quickly if one interview felt off in some way, so that Sasha could immediately let it go and enter the next one in a positive state of mind

And then we prepared a strategy for her talk. Presenting for an hour after two days of high-level interviews was a tall order. In terms of attitude, I encouraged her to see this as a great opportunity to share her work with people she respected in her field. Her research was legitimately cutting-edge and very exciting. I wanted her to internalize that she was already in the midst of an exciting journey and her talk was an invitation for others to join her.

I wanted her to get far away from feeling that her top priorities were to get the audience to like or approve of her. Yes, of course those things would be great. But they weren't empowering objectives for her to focus on.

As we got closer to the day of her talk, I could see that about halfway through rehearsal her energy was dropping because she was tired. This was completely understandable!

She had worked with a very talented designer and her slides were excellent. The graphics were colorful, fun, and helpful, and there wasn't too much text on them. At the halfway mark one of her slides had a rocket ship on it. I said, "When you see that rocket ship, that's when you need to dig deep and blast off. I know you won't have a lot of energy left, but you will be coming into the second half of your talk and you need to stay vibrant and engaged, even if you really want to take the longest nap of your life." That rocket ship became our little joke, so going forward, whenever she got to it, she would smile, dig deep, and summon her remaining energy for the rest of her presentation.

Her many, many years of hard work and commitment to her process paid off. She is now a full-time faculty member, continuing her groundbreaking research and teaching undergraduate students. She continues to present to secure grants, and this interview process serves as a great foundation for her future talks.

Smiling on the Phone Makes a Difference

Even when you can't be seen on a phone call, smile anyway. Smiling affects your vocal quality, makes your tone warmer and friendlier, and relaxes your face. Plus, your presence will be more welcoming and you'll be more relaxed.

Clothing

Your clothes can't put your slides together for you, but they can make a huge difference when it comes to your confidence. Please do not leave your clothing choice to the last minute! If you have been invited to speak at an organization you are not familiar with, make sure to ask the person who invited you what is appropriate in terms of dress. Wear colors and styles that match the occasion and make you feel good.

Dress Up or Dress Down?

It's better to err on the side of being a bit more dressed up than your attendees, rather than being the most casual person in the room.

If you have no idea or have gone through a recent change (in career, position, weight, or hair color), consider hiring a stylist to help you look your best. This professional may confirm what you already know, but they may also turn you on to styles that you never would have chosen to explore on your own.

If you have bought a new outfit for a presentation, try it on and rehearse in it. This will give you a chance to test drive it and see if it's the best choice. Also practice wearing the shoes you have chosen. If they are brand-new, be sure to break them in in advance. Sleek heels may look sharp, but pinched toes are really distracting and distractions are not what you need.

Figuring Out Your Color Palette

By factoring together your skin tone, hair, and eye color, you can find out your "season" and the best color palette for you. If you know that you are a winter, spring, summer, or fall, then you know exactly what colors look great on you. This is not astrology but instead a simple system that makes shopping easier. This website can help you figure it out: www.colormepretty.co.

Getting Comfortable Being on Camera

Presenting in front of a group of people can feel difficult enough, but doing it on camera can somehow make it seem even more challenging.

It can sometimes feel that because the camera is on you, this experience is all about you. But just like any other speaking event, it's not! Many of the same things that are true when you are onstage are true when you are on set or filming yourself in your home office. The experience is about your message and its effect on the audience. When you are in person, you can see the audience, so it makes it easier to remember this. When you are on camera, unless you are being filmed in front of a live audience, you will have to see them in your imagination. It can help to imagine a specific person you are trying to reach.

Here are some tips if you are speaking directly to a camera:

- **Sort out your technological issues.** Use a tripod to stabilize your camera or phone. It's best to have the lens approximately at eye level, about an arm's length away.
- **Look directly at the camera.** Picture who you are speaking to. I like to imagine one or two specific people, rather than picturing a vague crowd. If I were to record myself teaching a lesson on how to manage nerves when public speaking, I could imagine a person who is freaking out and really needs encouragement and strategies. Or I could picture a specific client who really struggled with nerves. The more specific I am, the better.
- **Wear colors and styles that look good on you.** Busy patterns can be a bit distracting, as can white clothing. Film yourself wearing your outfit to see how it looks on camera.
- **Lighting matters, as does your background.** It's important that your audience can see you, but you don't want to look washed out either. Have your light source be in front of you, not behind you. Along these lines, don't sit in front of a window to film. If the light source is behind you, you will be backlit and your face will be dark and the area behind you will be bright. Test to see how things look before doing a whole shoot. Make sure you are happy with the lighting and also with whatever is captured in the frame. Remove any

furniture or knickknacks that are distracting, like that funny poster on your wall. If you want your shoot to look really polished, it is worth it to get professional lighting advice. Also, gently wipe the lens of your camera with a lens-safe cloth to ensure a clear picture.

- **Shoot your video in a quiet room.** Close all doors and windows and turn off air conditioners and any other appliances that make noise. Be sure to test ahead of time to make sure that your sound quality is good and there aren't any distracting noises. If you are in a relatively empty room, there may be echoes, especially if you have high ceilings. If the room has more furniture and carpeting, this won't happen. You may want to invest in a simple lav mic to get the best sound possible. There is a range of options available, and some are very reasonably priced.

- **When rehearsing your script or outline, keep it conversational.** It may help to rehearse with someone so you can see what it feels like to say your message to a person. Keep your mind on your objective. What are you trying to accomplish and how are you trying to accomplish it? For instance, my objective could be to inspire my audience to eat more leafy greens. I could do this by using humor, by educating them on the benefits, or by enticing them by describing a delicious recipe. When I focus on these things, then I will be less tempted to worry about…me.

- **Keep your notes close by.** You can create a simple bulleted list and put it near the camera so you can easily reference it.

- **Know how to handle off-camera hosts.** If you are being interviewed for a documentary or anything along those lines, you may be interacting with someone despite being the only one on camera. The other person is "offscreen." In this case, you wouldn't directly look at the camera; you would look only at the person you are speaking with. This doesn't mean you have to stare at them constantly. You can make eye contact and also look away when you are thinking—just avoid looking directly into the camera. If you are on a set and it is unclear where to look, ask the director for guidance.

Activity: Create a Short Video Using Your Phone

It's very likely that you have a video camera on your phone, so the good news is that you can practice on your own. This activity is a chance to get comfortable being on camera. Your mission? To make a simple advice or how-to video.

1. Decide on a topic. Choose something that you can explain off the top of your head. It could be as simple as sharing a recipe you know by heart or demonstrating tying your shoelaces.
2. Determine who would benefit from your advice or instructions.
3. Think of three to five points or steps you want to get across.
4. Practice.
5. Wear an outfit you like. Find a quiet room. Figure out what your background will be.
6. Use a tripod or find a way to prop up your phone so the lens is right around eye level and you can easily turn it on and off.
7. Do a ten- to twenty-second test to make sure you like your outfit, the lighting, the sound quality, and your "set."
8. Adjust whatever you need to until you are happy with it.
9. Action! Record yourself and go through your talk a few times. Remember, you are speaking to a specific audience. This is about reaching them, not getting your lines to be perfect.

10. Watch it, see what is working, make adjustments, and then film a few more takes.

11. Share what you've created to get further feedback or simply... delete it. This will leave room for future videos!

When You Review Your Work, Observe and Be Kind

When you first watch yourself on screen, you may be tempted to be very critical of your appearance or any habits you discover (blinking or swallowing too much, scrunching up your forehead). You are most likely used to seeing yourself directly in front of a mirror, so different angles of your face may be a surprise to you—but they are not a surprise to anyone else. If you realize that certain colors or styles don't look good on you, or you need more or less makeup or better lighting—great! You can adjust those things. If you are very self-critical, seek out a more objective opinion of how you look from someone you trust. Becoming aware that you have a distracting tic or two will lead you toward addressing and correcting them. If you approach filming yourself with patience and a sense of humor, you will learn a lot, avoid tears, get the job done faster, and have better results.

Specific Circumstances

Different circumstances and venues require different public speaking strategies. In this section I'll share tips on approaching a variety of common situations so that you can more confidently approach new experiences. You can find entire books on some of these topics, but the information here is a good starting point.

For some of these scenarios, such as a wedding toast or a eulogy, you can prepare by writing and practicing exactly what you want to say. In other instances, like networking events and Q&As, you are less in control of exactly what might happen. You still can and definitely should prepare, but for your interactions to be organic and authentic, it's important to go with the flow as much as possible.

I've arranged the following public speaking opportunities in order from most formal and scripted to loosest and most improvisational.

Get Creative with Your Toast

If there is a really quirky thing about your friend that you love, incorporate it into your speech. For example, if he loves obscure movie references, start your speech with a relevant offbeat film quote. If she's a sports fanatic, creatively weave in sports metaphors or stats. I read about a couple who incorporated zombies into their vows in a funny yet meaningful way! Here's a great website for inspiration: https://offbeatbride.com/wedding-vows.

Toasts for Weddings and Other Special Events

You may be wondering how your beautiful relationship with your best friend or sibling has suddenly led to you having to write a speech and deliver it in front of family, friends, and random people you don't know. You've potentially spent thousands and thousands of hours together and now you are expected to piece together a short but coherent narrative that somehow honors your friendship, who the bride or groom is, their relationship, and their marriage. No problem, right?

It's understandable that this task can feel overwhelming. At this point you have a choice. You can decide that this experience is about lovingly sharing your perspective on how you and your friend have faced this crazy thing called life together. You can share with the community how you see your friend's qualities making them a great life partner, and how their relationship with their significant other has changed them for the better.

Or you can choose to make this experience about needing to get it right and impressing the audience. That sounds a lot more stressful, less fun, and less meaningful. Determine an intention that feels empowering to you. You can be guided by love or controlled by fear. I vote for love. I also vote for not leaving this till the last minute.

Activity: Write a Toast

In the following steps I outline how to write a toast. Most often these come up at weddings, but my instructions can generally be applied to toasts at retirement events, anniversaries, and other celebrations.

Step 1: Brainstorm

1. Let's start by brainstorming. When you have no idea where to start—or when you have too many ideas—it's helpful to cut to the core and create some structure. Here are some ways that you can jump-start your brainstorming process:

    • List all of the reasons why you love and/or admire the person you are toasting.

- Describe their vibe.
- List all of the reasons why you love/enjoy your relationship with this person.
- If it's a wedding toast, list all of the things that you enjoy and respect about their relationship with their fiancé.
- Read over your lists and see if there are any themes or patterns that emerge. Write those down.

2. List any appropriate stories that come to mind that help encapsulate what you have listed.
3. Say each of those stories out loud to yourself or to a friend who enjoys brainstorming. One of you can take note of the quirky details and fun phrasings that you come up with. You never know where one of these stories may lead you, so just let your memories guide you. Trust that you'll discover gems during the process.
4. You may want to sit with what you've discovered for a few days. Creativity and insights may float in when you're doing the dishes or when you're in your three p.m. meeting. Keep a little notebook with you to jot down ideas that come to you throughout the day, email them to yourself, or leave yourself voicemails. Trust that part of your brain is sifting through all that you have listed already and is making connections.
5. Gather your notes, lists, etc. Look them over and jot down any new ideas that emerge. It's best to do this when you have some downtime and can work uninterrupted. I realize that this may not always be possible, so do the best you can.
6. Which stories and anecdotes best flesh out the lists you created during step 1?
7. Have any interesting themes or patterns emerged?

Step 2: Create an Outline and Draft

1. Start to draft a potential outline. See what makes sense for the beginning, middle, and end. You can reshuffle these if you suddenly have a new idea about the order. If you're discovered any themes or patterns, could these appear in the beginning, middle, and end? One client of mine realized during his brainstorming process that "awkward first meetings" was a pattern, so he incorporated this theme throughout his speech.
2. Try doing a messy run-through out loud based on your loose outline. Take note of which parts flow and which parts need some transitional help. Jot down any new thoughts.
3. Keep playing with your talk until you are happy with the order and the flow. If you have time, let it sit for a few days to marinate.
4. Now it's time to refine what you've got. Let your original lists guide this process, and cut whatever seems extraneous.
5. Decide what kind of notes will best serve you. You could:

    *   Draft a script that you will read word for word. (Keep in mind that the more you rehearse, the more familiar you will get with your script, and the more conversational and natural it will be.)
    *   Create an outline or bulleted list to guide you.
    *   Whichever you choose, using a large font will make rehearsing easier.

6. Make a choice and test it. Practice with your script or outline to see if it's the right fit.
7. Choose the option that feels the best.

Step 3: Rehearse

1. Rehearse on your own and then with a safe friend, family member, coach, or all of the above. Rehearsing will help you to:

   - Get comfortable using your script or outline
   - See if any new ideas come to you and incorporate them into your draft
   - Discover if your transitions work
   - Get comfortable being on your feet and using your hands

2. If you don't yet know if you'll be using a microphone or if you will need to project, this is a good time to find out and practice accordingly. (Check out Chapter 4 for tips on both.)
3. Refine your notes to create a final draft or final outline and rehearse using that.
4. As the day of the event gets closer, remind yourself of your motivation and your love for your friend, sibling, or colleague. Let that guide your emotions.

Real-World Example:
A Very Shy Maid of Honor Creates a Heartfelt Speech and Nails It

Jill, a lovely young woman who was a shy introvert, came to me a few months before her best friend Isabelle's wedding. She was the maid of honor and had a lot of anxiety in anticipation of her toast, which made writing difficult. Jill and Isabelle had been best friends during middle school and high school but since then had gone to different colleges and then to different cities. They kept in touch, but each had developed new circles of friends. Jill felt that she didn't know how to go about writing this speech, given that most of their friendship had taken place years ago. Additionally, she had met Isabelle's fiancé, Dave, only a few times.

We discussed what this experience was really about at its core. It was an opportunity for Jill to express her love and gratitude for Isabelle's friendship over the years. She could speak about Isabelle's beautiful and quirky qualities in a way that no one else could. I knew that if she could tap into the joy of those memories, it would dampen her fear. I also assured her that it was okay if she didn't know Dave that well. She could speak about how he had made Isabelle's life better and happier.

Jill came up with several funny, sweet stories that captured Isabelle's personality and their friendship. She ultimately chose the ones that either made her laugh the hardest or moved her deeply. She also wrote about Isabelle's feelings for Dave and the ways in which she could see that they were a wonderful fit for each other.

Jill rehearsed and edited her script, and then rehearsed some more. On the big day she took some deep breaths and nailed it. (And she even got some laughs.)

Eulogies

Let's get this out of the way first: it's okay if you cry while giving a eulogy. You may not want to and you may not, but it's okay if you do. Everyone will understand. Events like funerals and memorial services often have a somewhat traditional structure to them, whether they are religious or not. But make no mistake: even though there is a beautifully put-together service with a neatly typed program, in the midst of it all is the vulnerable human spirit, with its ever-changing emotional life. It's nothing to be ashamed of or embarrassed about. Just remember your tissues.

If you are giving the eulogy, you have been given the honor of sharing about the deceased from your perspective. This is a chance for the audience to cherish what was unique, special, and wonderful about the person who has passed. Writing a eulogy for a loved one who has just died is a unique challenge. Your emotions may be all over the place, or you may be feeling drained—it's all okay. This task may actually assist you in your healing process.

One way to get started is by listing all the words that describe the person. Were they generous and thrifty? Always kind and always late? Once you have gotten those qualities down on paper, see if you can think of a story or two that captures much of the list. Sketch out your story, including a beginning, middle, and end. It may be a humorous story, a serious story, or an inspiring story—or a mixture of all three.

You may have many loving memories of the person in question. However, sometimes that's not the case. You may be called upon to give a eulogy for someone you had a difficult relationship with or someone who had a very troubled life and never fully resolved things before they died. There are ways that you can graciously acknowledge and handle this in the eulogy. Honoring what was true about the deceased can be done without turning the eulogy into an angry rant with lurid details that trigger everyone gathered. There may be people present at the service whose relationship with the person was really positive, so less is more when it comes to eulogizing a complex character. Speaking generally is the best bet:

- "Carl had a difficult start in life and faced many challenges. Sometimes he responded wisely; sometimes he really did not."

- "Dawn struggled with addiction for much of her life. This was a painful situation for her and especially for her loved ones, who did all they could to help her."

This acknowledgement may be healing for those present by validating their experience with the deceased. This approach will help you to represent the whole person to the audience, and not just sugarcoat everything.

Real-World Example:
Julie Creates a Deep, Rich, and Funny Eulogy for Her Beloved Sister

Julie came to see me to coach her in preparation for her sister's memorial service. The service was being held about six months after her sister, Michele, had passed away at too young an age from cancer.

She wanted to honor and celebrate her sister's memory, acknowledge all of the support Michele and family had received while Michele was sick, and also bring some lightness into what felt like a very tragic circumstance. Julie expressed that she was worried about crying while speaking and wanted to get comfortable with speaking publicly. She didn't have much experience, and this would be a very special occasion.

I often learn a lot from my clients, and this coaching experience was no exception. Julie had already created a PowerPoint for her eulogy. I was blown away by how she used this application traditionally reserved for business to beautifully recount how unique her sister was using funny imagery and amazing timing. Her slides did what she feared she could not.

I had never met her sister, but I will never forget what I learned about her! She was a veterinarian, had always loved animals, and was very much their advocate.

Here is a short passage from the eulogy demonstrating how Julie's PowerPoint helped elevate her story.

"If you knew Michele, you knew she was just a really nice person. I have a theory about how she got that way.

"You all know the story of

(Julie clicks to reveal the next slide.)

"Spider-Man. *(The slide has the image of cartoon Spider-Man.)*

"Peter Parker, a typical nerdy teenager, is bitten by a spider and acquires spider traits, like:

- "Spinning webs,
- "Having superhuman strength and reflexes,
- "As well as altered agility,
- "And the ability to wear skintight Lycra bodysuits.

"Well, when Michele was a toddler, she was attacked by a dog. It bit her in several places, even leaving scars. I have always speculated that that was when she took on the traits of your favorite family dog:

(Julie reveals the next slide. It is an image of a dog.)

- "Sweet,
- "Loyal,
- "Fun and funny,
- "Never held a grudge,
- "Always happy to see you, and
- "Pleased just to spend time with you...
- "But without the annoying fur clogging up the vacuum."

This was such an unexpected and awesome analogy. And it really fit. It was memorable, moving, and funny, all the elements that Julie wanted in her eulogy.

She rehearsed her well-crafted speech. I coached her on how to play with pauses, pacing, and other elements of vocal variety to make the serious moments more poignant and the jokes even funnier. With each run-through Julie became more comfortable. She was more connected to her words and what they expressed, which made the experience more intimate, personal, and rich.

As for her concerns about crying, I assured her that it was okay if she cried. No one would be shocked or surprised if she got tearful and sad, and they also may be reaching for tissues. Once she accepted that she couldn't know in advance if or when she would get emotional, she relaxed, was less tense, and became more self-accepting. (Also, Julie had a lot of humor in her eulogy, which had the potential to uplift her and the audience.) Whatever happened in the moment was okay.

Panels

Speaking on a panel is a great way to share your expertise and make some new connections. If you are invited to be part of a panel, you probably know what the topic of interest will be. Here are some tips on how to make the most of your experience:

- See if you can obtain the questions that the moderator will be asking in advance so that you can be focused as you prepare. Research who else will be on the panel with you and get a sense of why each of you was invited to take part. Maybe the moderator is hoping for a lively debate on a topic and so has invited panelists representing very different viewpoints. The moderator may organize a conference call with all participants to prepare for the panel, or you could initiate connecting with your fellow panelists to get ready by brainstorming together.

- What do you want your audience to learn from you? What are the interesting stories that capture what you want to get across? Are there any helpful tips? Is there any behind-the-scenes inside scoop that would be fun to share? Rehearse your narrative out loud. Include humor! Brainstorm and rehearse several different introductions to your stories so you can be flexible with your segues. Also, determine how you will unpack the different elements of your narrative and how you will close.

- Get there early to find out if you will have a mic, make sure your mic is working, and test out where you will be sitting. Have water handy and mute your phone.

- Sit in your chair—BIG, OPEN, and DIRECT. This will help you to stay confidently engaged. If you are going to wear a skirt or dress, make sure it's going to work well with how you are sitting—you may be on a high stool or a low, comfy armchair or sofa, or you may be behind a table.

- When it is time for you to share, bring the audience into your world. Remember your passion for the topic and why they will be served by hearing your insights and expertise.

- Be generous with your fellow panelists. If you've done your homework, you may have some creative ideas as how to take certain conversations further. If one panelist has been quiet for a while, find a way to engage them. Be conscious of not taking up too much time.

- Don't rush to answer questions. It's okay to take a moment to think about your answer.

Q&As

Often Q&As (question-and-answer sessions) occur after a presentation, reading, or film screening. Questions are asked that are related to the program that just happened. It's really helpful to repeat the question that was just asked—not only does it ensure that the whole audience hears the questions, but it also buys you time to formulate your answer!

Similar to the panel advice, don't rush to answer. It's okay to take a moment. It's also okay to acknowledge that you don't know the answer and you'd be happy to get back to that person later if they share their contact information with you.

People love stories, so always have a few in your arsenal. Stories about how you came up with your idea or crazy challenges you faced during the journey work well.

A Q&A always works best if you have a moderator to field the questions or, in some cases, to generate the first few questions to warm up the crowd. They can also help clarify any confusing questions.

Sometimes people ask questions that are only tangentially related to the subject at hand. (A friend of mine is convinced that people do this to show off their own knowledge on the subject.) You can graciously offer to get back to the person and then redirect the discussion to the actual topic. You can also remind the person that there are other people with questions and you have only a limited amount of time.

Webinars

It's wonderful that we can reach people remotely and share information via a webinar. But it's harder to get a read on the audience when you can't see their faces or body language. You are hoping they are fully engaged in your slides, but you can't really know if the participants are also baking brownies or organizing their home office during your training.

The same tenets are true online as in person: the more present you are, the more likely your audience will stay present with you. The more engaging you and your slides are, the more likely your audience will engage with you.

Even though it may feel like you are speaking into a void, you are not. You probably have a script, but please do not just read it. This will not help you to connect with your audience. It's important that you be alive and fully engaged, as though they are in the room with you. Make sure you rehearse! It may be tempting to think the stakes are lower because you are not seen, but people out there still need your expertise presented clearly.

Think of the type of person who could most benefit from what you are talking about. What stress are they under? What pain, challenges, and frustrations are they facing? When you get clarity on these things, then you will communicate via your computer to that person you are trying to help. This will also help you to remember that even though it's potentially just you and your laptop in the room, this webinar is not about you. It's about the value you can bring to your audience, so keep your attention on that goal.

Your intentions affect your tone. When you are on the phone with any kind of customer service rep, you can pretty quickly detect when someone is fully present and being genuine or when they are not. When your intentions are to help, it will affect the tone that those logged on to your webinar receive.

Podcasts or Radio

If you've been invited to be a guest on a podcast or radio broadcast, there are a number things to keep in mind. Speaking on a podcast or on the radio is different than other media because you are usually talking to only one or two people—host(s) or another guest—in a very intimate way. Even if you are calling in from a different location to participate, you are usually engaging in a one-on-one conversation led by the host. I spoke to Dominik Doemer and Shira Rascoe, who produce the Scholars Strategy Network's podcast *No Jargon*. They shared the following great tips with me about what to do during a podcast or radio show:

- **Tell lots of stories!** Podcasts work best when they can take a listener on a journey, and that's why many popular podcasts are story-focused. You'll want to have concrete examples and ideally real-life stories prepared in order to make your point and engage the listener.
- **Use visual and active language.** Paint a scene for the listener with your words. Describe what you're talking about in a way that allows the listener to imagine it. Art Hennessey, co-host of the *What Was That, Now?* podcast (and my husband!) offers this advice: sometimes there will be a live *YouTube* feed of the podcast. But if there isn't, remember that your audience won't be able to see you. This means that if you do any physical actions during the podcast, your audience will not see them. If during the show your host holds up a funny sign or you compliment your host on their T-shirt, describe to your audience what has just happened or what you are seeing.
- **Remember your tips to avoid *um* and *ah*.** These stick out a lot in podcasts since they are audio only. Similarly, try to avoid lip smacks, since they can come across very loudly in a podcast.
- **Slow down.** Don't speak too fast, because podcast listeners have only your voice to guide them. There is no text scrolling at the bottom of the screen, closed captioning, images, or video to help

listeners follow along. All they have is your voice, so give them time to digest it.

- **Don't be afraid to get personal, be goofy, or laugh.** These very human interactions often make for great audio. Joke around a bit with the host if you can, or share something personal if you're comfortable.
- **Embrace the pause.** Don't be afraid to take a short pause to collect your thoughts when answering a question. That's how you start out strong. The pause will help you avoid saying *um* or other fillers, like "That's a good question." (It's okay to say this, but use it sparingly.)

Video Conferencing—Zoom/Skype

Perhaps the most awkward part of videoconferencing is figuring out where to look. Where should you look?

- A. At the person on the screen
- B. At the camera, so it really looks to the viewer like you are looking at them
- C. At yourself

The answer is…B. Spend most of your time doing this—directing your attention to the camera. Look at the screen occasionally to see the facial expressions and body language of the person or people you are talking to.

It's wise to determine if your background, lighting, sound, and appearance are the way you want them before everyone else logs on. What's cool about these modes of communication is that you can take charge of your background and create a nice set for yourself that matches your goals for the session—professional, casual, personal, etc. The section "Getting Comfortable Being on Camera," found earlier in this chapter, gives you many more great tips for being on video.

Leading Meetings

Here are two lists that will guide you—what you can control and what you can't—in regard to leading meetings.

What You Can Control

These tips illustrate the various ways to be fully present during the meeting.

- **Plan ahead and strategize.** Know your audience, and try to anticipate their questions and needs.
- **Work out logistics.** If there are two or more members of your team participating, determine who will speak on what topic and when. Also, determine in advance who will take questions on each possible topic. (It can work well when one person leads the meeting and the other person or people take the floor less often.)
- **Respect everyone's time.** Do your best to start and end on time.
- **Deal with wild cards.** If new and important issues come up that are not on the agenda, you can best serve the group by finding out if it is critical to face this new concern now or table the new issue for a future date.
- **Guide the conversation, rather than control it.** You never know when a new great idea may emerge.

- **Put your best foot forward.** Your interaction at the meeting will represent what the client or audience can expect from you and your company in the future. You can represent your brand well…or not.
- **Tie up loose ends.** If you promised to follow up with a task after the meeting, do it!

Real-World Example:
A Team Creates Engaging Narratives to
Explain the Work They Do

A number of members of a division of the City of Escondido, California, attended one of my workshops to help them prepare for a presentation at an upcoming annual conference. The members were scientists whose essential work affected their community every day. Though a critical part of the ecosystem of their area, this division worked quietly behind the scenes. They received attention when something went wrong, rather than when things were running smoothly.

A number of people would be participating in the presentation. Members of the team did not often present in public, so we discussed nerves and how to handle being the center of attention, and explored empowering body language. We then focused on storytelling so the participants could develop personal narratives about their work. Each member of the team got up and spoke about what most excited them about their role. As they connected to their passion for the impact they were making in Escondido, I could see their confidence increase. One man shared his feelings of satisfaction and pride that his efforts made life safer for his son and the other kids in the Escondido school system. At the start of the workshop one woman had expressed anxiety about speaking publicly, but once she tapped into her passion for her scientific work, she became much more relaxed and fluid with her words. Other participants demonstrated how they would explain the value of their work to elementary and high school students. They brought creativity, humor, and warmth to their words that would engage their audience, no matter what age they were.

During our time together I learned a lot and gained a deeper appreciation for the work of divisions like theirs. My hope was that the attendees took away not only public speaking skills, but also an increased pride in their work. It can be easy to get caught up in the day-to-day tasks and frustrations of whatever job we do. Taking a step back and appreciating how our work makes an impact in our community can help build our confidence and recharge our batteries.

What's Not in Your Control

No matter how well you prepare for a meeting, you'll run into situations that are beyond your control. For example:

- People you anticipated attending the meeting instead send someone else on their behalf.
- New topics are introduced out of the blue.
- Participants have not read the materials you provided in advance.
- The technology doesn't work.

In these situations just do the best you can to keep the meeting on track and make the most of it. If the projector you were counting on is broken, for example, email your presentation to the client, hand out a few hard copies, or share it from a thumb drive. Also, revisit the strategies for dealing with snafus in the "Planning" section earlier in this chapter.

Introducing Yourself to a Group

Many people dislike having to introduce themselves to a new group. As it gets closer to being their turn, they get self-conscious and so stressed that they are not really listening to the other people's introductions. Even though they know their own name, job title, and responsibilities, they still feel like they don't know how to gracefully handle this moment. It's a short public speaking moment that feels too long.

Introductions do not exist to torture you; they are simply a chance to connect with individuals and new team members who have similar goals. This is an opportunity for you to make a connection with colleagues and potential collaborators.

The next time you need to introduce yourself, determine the energy you want to bring to the moment and choose the body language and words that align with that. Aim for an introduction that's informative but casual: "Hi, my name is Zoe and I'm the videographer within our in-house production department. You may have seen the video with the crazy surfer—that's our work. If you think a video would be helpful for your project, shoot me an email and we can brainstorm." Your words are important, but so is your presence. If you are sitting or standing with body language that is CLOSED and TIGHT, it doesn't send out a message that you will be a confident, helpful, and creative collaborator. Be a generous host during your moment. Open up your body language so that you are OPEN, DIRECT, and BIG. Not only will you feel more confident, but your nonverbal language will communicate that you are friendly, approachable, and ready to collaborate.

Staying present in the moment will also help you. Instead of fretting over what you're going to say, really listen to those who are speaking before (and after) you. You'll be less distracted by your worries and you'll learn about the people around you, which is valuable.

Networking

Many people dread having to attend a networking event. Why? Not knowing how to talk about themselves or their work may be the issue. Or maybe they feel that the other attendees seem inauthentic and schmoozy, trying to unload as many business cards as they can while always looking for the next person to chat with.

It can be easy to see networking as an awkward, icky brag fest. But if you go into a networking event (or any situation where people ask, "What do you do?"), you can approach it with a "This is how I improve people's lives" framework. You will then come from a place of authenticity and strength and not desperation or boredom.

What is your goal for networking events? Is it to blanket the room with your business card or make a few genuine connections?

As with other public speaking opportunities, this experience doesn't need to be about you. Go to give, rather than to get. You can be of service to people in the room by connecting them to others. If you become aware that Person A and Person B have a similar cause or interest, introduce them to each other. "Person A, do you know Person B? She and I worked together on a Save the Whales campaign. Person B, doesn't your company deal with clean ocean technology?" In this situation you may not explicitly be telling people what you do, but you are still communicating information about yourself. Your action of connecting others can demonstrate that you are helpful, supportive, and really listening.

Activity: Create Your Own Networking Narrative

Having a good sense of what you want to say to new people you meet can take a lot of stress out of a networking event. To create a brief and conversational summary about your work, follow these steps:

1. List the problems you solve in your role.
2. List whom you help. It could be certain individuals and/or companies.
3. List how you solve their problems.
4. List the reasons why you are good at solving these problems.
5. List why you enjoy solving these problems.

Now that you have figured out your content, it's time to weave these facts into a coherent and compelling narrative. Here are a few ways to create one:

- "When (people you help) are dealing with (problems you solve), I help them by (what you do to solve the problems). I use my (qualities you possess). I love this kind of work because (why you love it)."
- "I help (people you help) to handle (problems you solve). (People you help) are often too busy or not qualified to do this for themselves. I have experience (qualities you possess), so I am able to (what you do to solve the problems). I really love this work because (why you love it)."

Play around with your wording and rehearse until it feels natural and easy to say. Figure out a few different ways to explain whom you serve, how you serve them, and why it's a great fit for your personality, background and/or skill set.

Real-World Example:
Judy Creates a Compelling Networking Narrative

As you network it's important to highlight what's interesting about your work. My client Judy did just that. Here is a story about how we framed her job in a way to make it accessible and compelling to those she spoke with.

For most of Judy's career she had served her clients from behind the scenes. Extremely detail-oriented, conscientious, and efficient, she provided excellent customer service. Judy wanted only the best for her customers. One day she was promoted. In order to be successful in her new role Judy would need to attend networking events to bring in more clients for her firm. Though she was excited about the opportunity to get out of her comfort zone, she was really anxious and overwhelmed at the thought of talking about herself and her work at events.

"My industry is so boring. No one is going to want to hear about it. What do I do?"

I firmly believe nothing needs to be boring. Anything and everything has the potential be interesting. One person can tell you about their recent shopping experience at Costco and make you crazy with boredom. But then a comedian on HBO describes their bizarre adventure at the very same store and it is absolutely hilarious. The key to creating an engaging narrative is to figure out what elements of your story will resonate with your audience. Once you've done this, then you highlight these as you communicate in a conversational and authentic way.

Judy's work involved helping business owners find the best service providers for a particular need. Business owners would often be overwhelmed by the bureaucracy, numbers, and stacks of mind-numbing forms involved in the process.

Forms, bureaucratic red tape, feeling overwhelmed, and frustration are not interesting—Judy was right about that. But what *is* interesting is that Judy knows how to navigate these forms, numbers, and red tape, and actually get stuff done. Not only is she very knowledgeable about her field, but she also loves researching options to get the right fit for her clients. She feels great when she is able to make the process (and those pesky forms) easy for people. Making business owners' lives much less stressful on this front is what makes her thrive.

That's what is interesting—Judy's approach and navigational skills. She is a stress and pain reliever. She is the eye of the storm, a superheroine. She decided that she could touch on these things when talking about herself:

- The Problems: The stress, overwhelm, and frustration people face when navigating bureaucratic service providers
- Her Solutions: Her superheroine skills—knowledge, experience, and attention to detail, as well as her love of helping people (especially entrepreneurs)

Judy didn't need to meet people and talk about "the subtle but critical changes in Form 45A2-WE34 blah, blah, blah..." Instead, she could share information about herself that could potentially resonate and add value. We created a short list of talking points:

- My job is to be a stress and pain reliever for small business owners.
- I know small business owners are juggling so much that they often don't have time to navigate all available information to find the best deals for their companies.
- I have many years of experience working in this field.
- I know the ins and outs of what is available and how to handle this industry's frustrating forms.
- I love making this process easier for my clients so they can focus on their mission.

We role-played with these points so she could authentically make them her own and be very conversational. She didn't need to say exactly the same thing each time. We didn't want anything to sound overly rehearsed or canned.

The topics covered in this chapter address the vast majority of public speaking situations you may find yourself in. If you run into one not on this list, remember the key components: your passion for the topic; your audience (specifically who they are and what they need); why what you are saying is important; relevant stories that illustrate the points you are making; a call to action, if applicable; rehearsal; and remember, it's not about you!

CHAPTER 7

Presenting—
Creating an Experience for
Your Audience

You've brainstormed, you've created an interesting talk, and you've arrived at a final draft or outline. You've rehearsed your words, incorporated vocal variety, and made empowering body language choices. Now it's time to get out there and speak!

There is an interesting saying about the making of a movie: there's the movie you write, the movie you shoot, and the movie you edit. When it comes to public speaking, there's the talk that you write, the talk that you rehearse, and then the talk (or experience) that you give to the audience. It's time to focus on the final part—creating a powerful experience for your audience.

This chapter will delve into the connection between you and those listening to you. You'll learn how to take them on an engaging journey and also how to get back on track if you lose your footing. I'll cover how empathy and gratitude can melt any resistance you may be facing, as well as how to handle eye contact and props.

How Your Intentions Affect Your Interaction with Your Audience

There are many recipes for brownies—some are incredibly complex and some are simple. For the least complicated box mix you just add water to the brownie mix, stir, and bake. The water is a crucial element, though. No water = no brownies.

This is similar to a live presentation. You, the speaker, are responsible for creating the mix. The audience is the water. The stirring happens when you and the audience come together and interact. You will be doing most, if not all, of the talking. But their presence matters. Without the audience, this experience cannot happen. There is an energetic exchange between the speaker and the audience that can only occur if the speaker is open to it.

Speakers are there to speak; the audience is there to listen. But the magic happens when the presenter genuinely connects with the audience, by really looking at them and speaking *with* them, rather than *at* them.

Entering the Stage with Presence

You can enter the stage passively, wondering what the audience's response to you will be. Or you can take the stage actively, sending out positive energy. (BIG, OPEN, DIRECT, and BRIGHT.) You don't have to be a huge personality to do this. Let your deep passion for your mission be your engine.

You are there to give a presentation, a pitch, or a toast. Let's focus on the verbs of that sentence, which let you know what to do—*are* and *give. Are* means you exist. You are present in the moment, existing. *Give* is a great reminder of your goal. You are giving to your audience.

You are giving your audience an experience, a journey, from point A to point B to point C and so on. The adventure you are guiding them on is intellectual and emotional.

Your question to yourself should never be: How are my words supposed to *sound*? No, the better questions are: Who do I want to affect? Why do I want them to know what I am telling them? Why does what I am saying matter? How do I want the audience to feel as I take them on this journey?

How many times do you think musical legend Bruce Springsteen has sung "My Hometown" in concert? A lot. Many, many, many, many times he has looked out at the crowd and sung that song. My guess is that he doesn't imagine that he is singing to yet another crowd in yet another city. I imagine that he has a sense of what his Boston fans are like, what his Kansas City fans are like, and what his Detroit fans are like. And he sings specifically to those specific individuals in that specific place at a specific time.

When Your Talk Lacks Engagement

I am always excited to listen to speakers tell their stories. I take note of how the experience affects me and what I take away from it. I want to see what moves me deeply, what inspires me to take action, and what really cracks me up.

I attended a conference in New England a few years ago. One afternoon an accomplished woman got up and shared her story about her career path. She had a physically demanding job in a male-dominated field. Very few women had ever had her specific job and she had a tremendous amount of responsibility.

Despite the great lessons she shared with us, I was surprisingly underwhelmed. I wasn't touched on a deeper level. When I thought about her accomplishments and stories intellectually, I could see how impressive they were. Yet viscerally, I wasn't hooked. I noticed that the audience was also not as engaged. Make no mistake, her talk was well-organized and made sense. She had vocal variety and was articulate, very confident, and well-dressed. This power player had a great message. But there was something about her delivery that kept her from nailing her speech.

What she lacked was genuine interaction with the audience.

Two years later I attended the same conference. This same woman was presenting and she delivered the same talk—in the exact same tempo and cadence as she had before. She also stressed the same words. She was in a vocal pattern, which can sometimes happen when people do the same talk, sales pitch, or lesson plan over and over again. Vocal patterns do not engage people, and again I was not deeply engaged with what she shared.

Imagine that you create a talk that is full of inspiration and humor and is really well written. But if you deliver it with vocal patterns, on autopilot, you will not make the impact you have the potential to make.

Engaged Customer Service People—You Know 'Em When You See 'Em

Have you had this experience? You are having issues with your cell phone bill or credit card and you call the company for assistance. A customer service professional answers the phone and it is clear that they are following a script incredibly closely. It feels more like you are interacting with a robot who needs an upgrade than a human being. While I appreciate that companies are doing all they can to ensure that their representatives provide polite and professional service, it can feel like the rep is not fully present. They have not yet made the words their own, meaning the words do not sound natural or authentic.

It is refreshing when you receive assistance from someone who is not only professional but also doesn't sound like they are highly scripted. It feels like a real interaction that is still polished, but the rep is totally present in the moment with you on the phone.

Use Eye Contact to Engage

When you know why you are giving your presentation and what message you wish to impart to your audience, it will become easier to make eye contact with your audience members. Look at individual members of the audience from time to time. (Please do not fixate on one friendly audience member for most or all of your talk, though; you will make them uncomfortable!) Remember, you are the host, and a good host will want to connect with as many of their guests as possible. This helps you build rapport and trust with them.

Eye Contact Helps Pacing Too

In addition to helping your audience to feel that you want to connect with them, eye contact can also serve to help you slow down. If you really look at individuals in the audience as you share with them, you will feel more grounded and not be tempted to talk too fast.

If you are not yet comfortable with direct eye contact, here's a trick: look at people's foreheads or noses. It will seem like you are looking in their eyes, but it's not as intense an experience for you. Over time you will become more comfortable and you will be able to connect via eye contact.

If you have audience members who are on their phones and not engaged at that moment, remember, you have no idea what is going on with them. They may be very rude or they may be dealing with an emergency or even taking notes. Focus on those who are fully present. Try to not allow those other folks to distract you.

If you are in an auditorium where bright lights are lighting you and the audience is in the dark, then eye contact with the audience is less of an issue. You will not be able to see them. Simply look out into the crowd and imagine that you are speaking with individuals.

The Key to Audience Interaction: Authenticity

I bet you can remember experiencing a simple and yet powerfully authentic moment. It may have happened during a brief interaction with someone you don't know that well—maybe your dental hygienist really seemed to care how you were doing. Or your friend who usually jokes about everything confided his feelings of self-doubt. When something is authentic, it is genuine and memorable.

Whether we are talking to our best friend, our financial planner, or a supermarket clerk, I believe most of us can sense when someone is genuine. Once, on a flight, a delightful steward asked me if I would "Care for a beverage today?"

I said, "Just water, please."

"Would you like ice? Or just the bottle?"

"Just the bottle, please."

"Here you are!"

"Thank you."

"You're welcome!"

That was the whole exchange. It was simple, but it inspired me to include it in this section. My thoughts after our quick interaction were: *This guy really likes his job! He authentically connected with me during this brief exchange that he has probably had a gazillion times this week alone. He was fully present and the interaction was very caring and sweet. I very much felt taken care of.*

There is a lot of inauthenticity all around us. We are more likely to trust someone when they are authentic. Imagine how authenticity will elevates your talk, toast, or interview. The key is candor and honesty. Mean what you say. Say what you mean. Be fully aligned with the goals of your talk.

Activity: Experiment with Intention

You can say the same set of words two different ways—one with authenticity and engagement, and one without—and create a totally different experience for your audience. Try this exercise to train yourself to speak with passion and engagement.

1. Sing or simply say the words to the birthday song out loud as though it was for some boring third cousin whom you hardly know at a big, lame family event.
2. Sing or simply say the words as though it was for an awesome friend or family member, one who is always there for you and makes you laugh like no one else.
3. What was your experience with each version?
4. Which one was more enjoyable to express? Why?

Real-World Example:
Lei Brings Her Authentic Personality to Her Inspiring Stories

Lei Wang is the first Chinese woman and the first Asian American to successfully complete the Explorers Grand Slam. This means that she summited Mount Everest, climbed six other formidable mountains, and skied to the North *and* South Poles.

You know, normal stuff.

By the time I met Lei she'd already written *After the Summit*, a book about the life-changing lessons she learned during her adventures. She was now gearing up for a career as a motivational speaker. One of the first things I noticed was Lei's passion for life and her great sense of humor. As she rehearsed in front of me, it was clear that she had great insights and fascinating stories. Her tone was kind and patient as she shared her challenges, frustrations, and victories.

However, while kindness and patience are lovely qualities, I was missing Lei's vibrant personality and humor. I wanted to be inspired by Lei's hard-won wisdom, but I also wanted to witness a full range of her emotions, from anger to despair to hope, as she guided her audience and me moment by moment through the highs and lows of her journeys. If audience members could appreciate her stories in a visceral way, they would appreciate her insights on a deeper level.

By working on her tone and shifting her physical movements on stage, Lei brought more colors, spontaneity, and humor to her presentation. As she relived the (literal) ups and downs of her climbing and skiing adventures, there was now a sense of immediacy to her words. Her physical movement also helped to underscore her high-stakes stories. These changes helped Lei stay present in each moment of her talk. This would compel her audience to stay present with her as well.

How to Handle the Energy in the Room

One of the biggest challenges that people grapple with when presenting is managing all of the stimuli in the room. The stimuli could be sounds, such as attendees chatting, or it could simply be the energy of the people present. Some people may be having a hard day, and you may sense their negative moods. Others may feel stressed because they have so much work to do and really wish they were at their desk plowing through their inbox. You are picking up on their anxiety.

When speaking with someone individually, you can tune in to their energy relatively easily, hearing their tone, seeing their expressions, and reading their body language. When your group expands to two or ten or fifty, it's impossible to tune in to each individual in quite the same way. There are too many stimuli. It's as if you are walking into a store that sells TVs and each one is on a different channel. It's easy to get overwhelmed if you don't have a game plan.

Think Like a Tree

To handle the energy of the crowd, whether it is quiet, chatty, friendly or challenging, you need to be grounded, focused, and strong. Let's take some cues from…trees. Trees, such as the sassafras, Japanese pagoda, and certain pines, put a lot of effort into developing deep taproots, roots that grow vertically downward. Subsidiary rootlets then grow from these taproots. During the trees' first years of life there is actually not a lot of top growth to be seen. Creating a diverse and deep root system is these trees' top priority and is where all of their energy is focused. In Parts One and Two you learned how to develop your own invisible root system, including:

- Your mission, your "why"
- Understanding what you can and cannot control
- Caring, but not too much
- Letting go of perfectionism

These "roots" are your anchors and they are vitally important.

Tree roots serve two vital functions: they gather nutrients from the soil and they support the weight of the top growth of the tree. The nutrients that *your* roots gather include:

- Anything that fuels your passion for your topic—research, conversations, etc.
- Positive beliefs
- Self-acceptance
- Support from your friends, family, or colleagues
- Preparation
- Writing

The deeper your roots, and the more plentiful the nutrients in the soil, the stronger you will be. Though we don't see your roots, we do see you, the tree. Your strong body language choices (BIG, OPEN, DIRECT) will give you strength and further ground you. A strong and deep root structure enables a tree to withstand heavy winds without being uprooted and toppling over.

I think of the stimuli from the crowd as winds in the air. If you stay rooted in your mission, you will be able to stay focused, even if the energy feels overwhelming. Instead of tuning in to each individual's energy system, crank up your own energy. Yes, you do want to have awareness if much of the audience seems bored or fidgety. Those could be cues to bring more energy to your delivery, or to mix up your pace, pitch, or pauses. But you don't have to be distracted by their energy.

And, believe it or not, dealing with stimuli will also strengthen you. We'll take another cue from the trees. Scientists have found that wind is a very important factor for a tree's growth and maturity. When wind blows against a tree, it causes its root system to grow deeper, which supports the tree as it grows taller. If the tree never encounters any wind, the tree will collapse before it is fully mature. As for you, the more that you get up in front of a crowd and consciously dig into your roots, the stronger you will be. Keep expanding your belief systems, knowledge, and support systems throughout your lifetime. They will enable you to stand tall and handle any audience or circumstance that comes your way.

Dealing with Weeds

As you develop more confidence and self-acceptance, you may become aware of some weeds—negative people and situations in your life that don't support your growth. These people may be stuck or simply like creating drama. Be intentional about who has influence on you and your life.

When You Are Facing Opposition

Once in a while you may encounter opposition when speaking to an audience. Perhaps you are presenting innovative ideas or research that challenges the status quo. If you anticipate that your audience's belief systems are closed to your point of view, it can feel intense and scary to take the stage.

In these circumstances it is critical that you dig as deep as you can into that root system we just discussed. You need to stand solidly on your mission—your "why." It may be tempting to feel defensive when facing a group like this. But raising your defenses—even just by closing your body language—will not serve you.

A police officer, Matt, attended one of my workshops. As part of the lesson on body language each participant role-played a scenario. When it was Matt's turn, I told him to enter the room and introduce himself as though he were visiting a high school in a neighborhood where many people have negative feelings about the police. I instructed the rest of the class to close their body language and be very suspicious of him when he appeared. When Matt entered the room, we could see that his defenses were up. He was anticipating opposition and trying to protect himself by closing his body language. When I asked the class how they responded to him, they said they felt their own defenses and skepticism increasing.

I had Matt enter the room again. This time his physicality was OPEN, BIG, and DIRECT. When he introduced himself to the group, his tone was friendly and warm. The class reported that as a result of his openness, they felt their own defenses start to melt.

Your audience might not initially be open to you or your message. But this does not mean you need to be closed to them. It may feel vulnerable to be open, but it's worth it. The only way innovation and progress can happen is when the usual way of thinking and behaving is challenged.

*"I can't understand why people are frightened of new ideas.
I'm frightened of the old ones."*
—John Cage

Conveying Empathy and Gratitude

If your goal is to talk *with* your audience, rather than *at* them, then fostering a sense of "we" is a good idea. You can do this by including empathy and gratitude in your communication.

Dealing with the Unexpected in an Empathetic Way

When you acknowledge what is true, unusual, or unexpected about what is happening, you stay present to what is true in the moment. Your audience is much more likely to be receptive to you when you are present. Perhaps:

- Your meeting is happening at a freakishly early or late hour.
- Your team has to unexpectedly work for many weekends in a row to make a deadline.
- There is a championship sporting event (the Olympics or World Cup) happening at the same time.

Acknowledging these circumstances, whether they are annoying, frustrating, or exciting, will help your audience to stay focused on you and your message. Here are some examples of addressing what is true with empathy and gratitude:

"Thank you for meeting at this unusually early hour—I know it's still dark outside. I have brought us all coffee. We're meeting now because it's really important that we discuss X before the nine a.m. board meeting today."

"I know the Red Sox are playing the Yankees right now, which is really distracting for us all. It's important that we meet right now so we can cover X before the weekend. If we can really focus now, I'll do my best to finish up quickly so we can catch the end of the game."

"I know we have worked every weekend this month to meet our deadline. I know this was not the original plan and that everyone has had to sacrifice a lot to keep the project on track. I appreciate all of your efforts and commitment to make this work. As you know, this project is really important for our client and also the future of our company. Your hard work is moving us forward and there is light at the end of the tunnel. And the company will be paying for a fancy lunch to be brought in today."

In each example you are helping your audience or team to know that they are valuable and why their sacrifice matters. If people know that their efforts, and especially their extra efforts, are noticed and appreciated, they are much more likely to give their all for the larger vision.

Something may happen that you weren't expecting. If you don't address it, whatever it is that's happening will distract your audience. Perhaps:

- There is unexpected weather, such as a raging blizzard that is worse than was predicted.
- There is loud music playing nearby.
- The room has become unusually warm or cold.

Here are some things you could say:

"I am noticing that the snow is getting really intense outside. Let's take a quick break to check the weather and see if we need to wrap this up for today and get home before it gets worse."

"I am hearing loud music next door, which is distracting. Let me pause for a moment and see what's happening."

"Is anyone else feeling that the room is really cold? Yes? Let me see if I can adjust a thermostat or call someone who knows how to turn on the heat."

In these situations, though it may not feel ideal to stop, it is wise to take charge of the unforeseen circumstance and be a leader. In the instance of the snowstorm you may have parents in the room who are suddenly worried about early school closures. It will be difficult for them to concentrate on what you are sharing with them until they have more information. Be a good host for your guests and take care of them.

Being Sympathetic

What if your client starts crying during a meeting? Let's say you are a real estate agent and a former client has called you to say that her husband has just died and she has to sell her house. While on the phone, she breaks into tears. You may need to get practical information from her before you can move forward, but in this moment simply be present with her. "I'm so sorry, Linda." Give her some space to talk if she wants to. You don't need to become Linda's therapist, but you can be an empathetic listener. After she shares, you could say something like,

"Again, I'm so sorry, Linda. I know this is an overwhelming time. Why don't I check back in with you next week and we can take it from there? I'll do research on my end and gather a list of questions for the next time we talk. How does that sound?" By communicating in this way, you're staying present to all that is true in the moment. Linda needs to sell her house and needs your help. She is devastated and overwhelmed, and she needs reassurance and guidance. Your words can assure her that she has started making a bit of progress with her goal and that you will be making efforts on her behalf while she takes care of other more pressing matters. Your empathy during this very dark moment will help her feel taken care of.

Having a Growth Mindset

There may be days when it's clear that your talk, meeting, or other experience made its mark. The audience was fully engaged and laughed at all the right moments, you had a blast, and people wanted to continue discussing the topic with you afterward. There may also be days when some things feel great and other aspects are just "meh." And then there are those experiences after which you need the solace of ice cream. As you compassionately assess your experiences, take note of what you sense didn't work so great as well as what went beautifully. Yes, your role is to share information in a compelling way so others can learn, but you also have an opportunity to learn and grow. If it is appropriate, see if you can debrief with someone you trust who was at the event. They may be able to shed light on things in a helpful way. There may be interpersonal dynamics or issues relating to organizational culture that have nothing to do with you affecting the vibe in the room.

We all have seasons in our lives that are marked by extreme difficulty, be it the death of a loved one, loss of a job, or health issues. When we interact with coworkers, clients, prospects, or even bosses when they are struggling, being present with compassion is a loving choice.

Anticipating Potential Issues

The examples I have listed so far are regarding unexpected or unusual situations we are responding to with empathy. There is also a way to be proactive. Do your research on your clients, prospects, or partners so you can understand what's going on in their worlds. Have they recently had layoffs? Have their stock prices gone down? Factors like these will help you understand and empathize with the challenges they are facing. You'll comprehend why certain decisions they are making are difficult—perhaps because of budget or staffing reasons. Understanding an individual's role in their organization will also help you understand where their stress comes from.

Supportive Silence Can Communicate a Lot

If you are with a team while they are mulling over a big decision, such as choosing a new location or deciding on a new marketing campaign, it's important to be present and have empathy as the individuals ponder the pros and cons and ride their emotional waves. Big decisions can paralyze some people, while others make them on a whim and never look back. It's important to realize that groups are made up of people who process information very differently from one another. Showing patience and giving people their space will be appreciated in the long run. Not everyone is going to be happy with every decision, but people want to at least feel as if their opinion has been heard.

Land It Like a Gymnast

When I watch the Olympics, I am blown away by what athletes are capable of. I love watching the gymnasts. I don't fully grasp all of the nuances of an amazing acrobatic feat, but I know when they stick the landing. The gymnast's feet are solidly on the ground and they boldly raise their arms in the air, enjoying a brief moment of stillness after a tremendous amount of athletic daring.

When you are presenting, your points will be more memorable if you stick the landing. End your sentence decisively before moving on to your next slide or concept, and especially when you finish your presentation. You will avoid having your ideas all blend together if they have clear beginnings and endings.

Here's an example of landing the last sentence of a talk about taking care of curly hair:

"So, remember, if you have curly hair, it's best to blot your wet hair with a cotton T-shirt, rather than using a towel to roughly dry it. This will keep your curls intact and prevent frizz. There are times in life when the best strategy is to go with the flow. *(start to slow down)* When you have curls, going with the flow—letting your curls do their thing—*(slow down these last words more)* is the best bet for a beautiful look."

Capture Their Imagination—One Moment at a Time

When people come to a meeting, conference, or wedding, they are coming from the activity and noise of their own lives into a new circumstance. Your job as a presenter is to continually be present and capture your audience's imagination so that they remain with you in the moment and don't get pulled back into their own worlds.

You have been acquiring many tools to enable you to do this. You've learned how to:

- Prioritize your desire to make an impact over a need to impress others.
- Value your contribution.
- Think of yourself as a generous host.
- Accept any feelings you are having, such as nerves, and not make a big deal of them.
- Confidently stand, sit, and move.
- Express yourself with power and flair—using pitch, pace, volume, and pauses to entice your listener.
- Grab your audience's attention right at the start.
- Creatively use language in the form of stories, examples, and analogies to bring your audience on a journey with you into your world.
- Create compelling slides, notes, outlines, or scripts and know how to rehearse and present them.
- Inspire your audience to take action after your strong ending.

Great! Now it's time to bring all of this together to create an experience for your audience—one moment at a time. Your presence, energy, mission, words, and vocal choices will be the tools that you use. You will take your audience on an adventure that includes an emotional journey and also an intellectual one.

The energy generated by your thoughts is palpable to your audience. No matter what words you are using, your tone and body language will communicate your true attitudes loudly and clearly. This is called subtext. You will typically trust tone and body language over words.

To be really clear to your audience, you need to have your words, intentions, attitudes, and body language aligned so you are not sending out mixed messages. Remember, wanting to get it over with will rush you. People will miss valuable information and be less engaged in your story. Your attitude about everything will come through to your audience, whether you are conscious of this or not. For the best results, be aware and intentional.

When You Struggle to Believe Your Own Words

If I sense that a client is awkward or uncomfortable while they are practicing their talk in front of me, I'll ask them what is going on. Often I am picking up on the fact that they have mixed feelings about the data they are sharing or don't 100 percent buy into what they are saying. Their ambivalence is loud and clear and it undermines their message. Once the client makes peace with whatever has been distracting them, then their presentation flows smoothly. To get there the client may need to think more critically about the point they are making or dig deeper into the data or research so they can be confident with those parts of their message. They are then fully committed and present, which means their audience is more likely to trust them and keep listening.

Here are tips on how to engage your audience moment to moment:

- Be deliberate when you lay out the context of your talk at the beginning. This is what will give them an entry point to your world. (You don't want people to feel like they missed the beginning of a movie.)
- Create solid transitions from one idea, story, or slide to the next. You can build suspense, drama, comedy, or all of the above when

you slow them down and/or increase your volume. Transitional sentences often illustrate an "aha" moment or some sort of change or reversal. It is important that your audience follow you during your whole talk, and especially at the twists and turns of your narrative. Here are a few examples of transitional moments:

- "This is what we did next." (You could emphasize the words *this* and *next*.)
- "It was in that moment that I realized something." (You could emphasize the first *that* and *realized*.)
- "But this wasn't in the plan." (You could emphasize the words *but* and *this*.)

- Pauses are your friend. Use them sparingly, but a well-placed pause can make a great impact. Pauses allow what you've just shared to sink in. They can be an integral part of humorous misdirection. You could use one after a transitional sentence. And when you take your intentional pause, you also get a moment to catch your breath.
- Stillness is powerful. Embrace this when you are saying key points and during light-bulb, "aha" moments. This will bring the audience's focus to your words, rather than to any distracting movement.
- A variety of sentence lengths will help you to mix it up. Shorter sentences are more memorable and are great to use to break up a string of longer sentences.
- Don't take yourself too seriously. If something unexpected happens—you spill your water or lean up against a blackboard and accidentally get chalk all over yourself—stay light and loose. Just make a joke and get back on track with your mission. If you don't make it a big deal, you'll more easily be able to get your audience to refocus on your narrative.

How to Capture Audience Imagination When You Are Dealing with Dry Subject Matter

You might wonder if engaging your audience is possible if your topic is very dry. Yes! Anything can be made interesting. The feature film *The Big Short* does a great job doing this very thing. Though the collapse of the American economy in 2008 is a grim subject, this movie manages to be engaging, informative, and even fun. It covers dry, confusing, and fraudulent financial concepts, yet is very intentional about enabling the audience to enjoy their educational ride.

Here are some helpful ideas for being engaging even if your subject matter is incredibly dry:

1. **Speak *with* your audience rather than *at* them.** At different times throughout the film Ryan Gosling's character, Jared Vennett, looks directly into the camera and speaks with us, the audience. He sympathizes with the fact that we may be getting really bored with convoluted explanations of financial dealings. We feel he is with us in this story, rather than condescending to us, though we know he knows more than we do.

2. **Make surprising analogies.** Once Vennett (Gosling) senses our yawns and restlessness, the responsibility of explaining the details of the mortgage crisis falls to the gorgeous Margot Robbie, who is luxuriating in a tub. She certainly gets and keeps our attention. However, it is not only because she is in a bubble bath drinking champagne; it is also because she finds a simple, direct, and surprising analogy for what she is talking about. She equates subprime mortgages with…poop. And she is funny about it.

3. **Use props if it will help clarify a complicated process.** In the film Vennett has caught wind of how the historically

stable housing market is about to collapse. As he pitches to a group of investors, explaining to them why they should bet against the housing market, he plays with Jenga blocks. (Jenga is a game during which players build an increasingly unstable structure block by block.) This helps him to clarify a very counterintuitive position. He uses these blocks in a compelling way to explain this ticking time bomb.

People love visuals. If you have a suitable analogy that can be shown visually, through a simple prop, video, or picture, go for it.

How to Recover If You Get Lost or Find Yourself on Autopilot

If you find that you are distracted, feeling off track, or in a vocal pattern, there are several things you can do to come back to the present moment. Take a sip of water. This will give you a few moments to take a deep breath and collect yourself. You can also remind yourself why you are saying what you are saying. Also, try slowing down so you can make your points one at a time. Each of them matters; make them count. Finally, share your words as though you were speaking to one person who really needs to hear your message.

My husband, Art, was recently performing in a one-man show. During one performance an old trunk he was sitting on collapsed underneath him. It slowly and awkwardly sank to its demise. Once it finished its death rattle, Art was able to get back on his feet. He acknowledged the comical incident by laughing with the audience. He made a joke connecting the instability of the trunk with something in the show. Then he got very still, took a pause, and got back on track with the show. The audience stayed present with him the whole time, because he was able to stay present and take it all in stride.

CONCLUSION

My hope is that by reading this book you've been able to shift the negative thoughts and feelings you've had about public speaking and your potential to make a powerful and positive impact. As you prepare for your next opportunity, dig deep as you explore why your ideas matter to your audience. No one sees the world exactly as you do—share your concepts, data, and vision as creatively as you can. Own your space, stand tall, breathe deeply, be present, and speak with your audience. Now go out there and do great work!

Feel free to drop me a line and tell me how these ideas worked for you. I can be reached at amanda@bostonpublicspeaking.com. You got this!

ADDITIONAL RESOURCES

Books

Cameron, Julia: *The Artist's Way*

Duhigg, Charles: *The Power of Habit*

Gawain, Shakti: *Creative Visualization*

Huffington, Arianna: *The Sleep Revolution*

Lindor, Christie: *Release: Use the Power of Forgiveness to Get Unstuck and Thrive in Your Career*

Tolle, Eckhart: *The Power of Now* and *A New Earth*

Wang, Lei: *After the Summit: New Rules for Reaching Your Peak Potential in Your Career and Life*

Websites

Belly breathing with folks on *Sesame Street*: www.youtube.com/watch?v=_mZbzDOpylA

Diaphragmatic breathing tips: www.healthline.com/health/diaphragmatic-breathing#tips

Free photos to make your slides more powerful: https://unsplash.com/

Vocal fry information: www.hopkinsmedicine.org/health/articles-and-answers/wellbeing/is-vocal-fry-ruining-my-voice

ACKNOWLEDGMENTS

To all of my clients who allowed me to include their challenges and victories within these pages—thank you! You'll be an inspiration for others as they face their fears and walk big and sparkly.

Art—thank you for your encouragement, insights, humor, and culinary support!

Samantha—thank you for cheering me on! Mike, thanks for your story and support. Alex and Isabelle—you help me stay present and you're the best!

Eva Bilick—thank you for your very valuable feedback!

Kate Perry, Lei Wang, Christie, Eliza Ryan, Julie Barnard, Bryan Roof, Adrienne M. Politis, Nicki, Eva, Mercedes, Shira Rascoe, Dominik Doemer, Greg Maraio, CC Donelan, Oyuna Jenkins, Byron Odwazny, Sarah Shapard, Michael Giannone, and James Gardiner—you each contributed to this book in your own unique way. Thank you!

Melissa, Seana, Maria, and Jill—your wisdom has greatly impacted my life, my work, and this book.

Thank you to the awesome people who provided valuable feedback and support: Michele Crosby, Dan Sullivan, Ted Graffam, Christine, Rollyn, Mardie, Kate H., Dimitrous, Elisa, Sheryl, Doli, Rita, Carolyn, Lucy, Greg, Maggie, Roberta, Brian, Nick, and Rebecca.

Huge thanks to John, Scott, Will, Maura, Christie, Kate, Alexandra, Lei, and Imac for reading this book before it went to press.

Julia Jacques—I am incredibly grateful for your guidance and support throughout the writing process. It's been a joy to work with you.

Laura Daly—thank you for all your wisdom, and for letting my voice come through! I've loved working with you.

To everyone at Adams Media/Simon & Schuster—many thanks for helping my dream of writing this book come to pass!

INDEX

Modern Family, 136

Negatives, avoiding, 17, 34–35, 38–51, 60–61, 120–24, 172–75

Nervousness, 9, 12–14, 39–46, 51–54, 81–83

Networking, 205–9

"Never" statements, 51–52

New York magazine, 165

No Jargon, 199

Opposition, 221–22

Pacing, 49, 93–101, 159, 168, 195, 215, 221. *See also* Timing

Panels, 113, 171, 195–97

Pauses, 49, 94–101, 159, 168, 195, 200, 221, 229–31

Perfectionism, 13, 23–25, 55–59, 220

Perry, Kate, 165–66

Physical empowerment, 63–83, 202–4, 211, 220–22

Pitch variation, 91–92, 95–99, 159, 168, 221, 229

Podcasts, 113, 118, 198–200

Positives, 16–17, 34, 40–52, 118, 171–79, 192

Preparation
emotional preparation, 42–62
for interviews, 25–26, 58–59
mental preparation, 42–62

for presentations, 12–13, 31–62, 171–209

Presence, 31, 35–40, 63–64

Presentation. *See also* Public speaking
beginning, 34, 130–33, 164, 229–32
empowering, 31–83, 85–115, 202–4, 211, 220–22
ending, 139–40, 149, 164, 228–31
memorizing, 118, 155–62, 166
perspective on, 17–22
preparation for, 12–13, 31–62, 171–209
rehearsing, 26, 32, 112–19, 145–57, 165–85, 189–98
tips for, 29–62, 75–77, 117–233
visualization of, 118, 133, 171, 175–76

Projection, 88–90, 96

Public speaking. *See also* Presentation
defining, 13–15
fear of, 9, 13–19, 23–25, 40–43
perspective on, 17–22
success with, 10, 18–20, 27, 57, 163
types of, 9–10, 13–16

Q&A sessions, 111, 135, 150, 197

Radio broadcasts, 198–200

Rascoe, Shira, 199

Ratatouille, 134

Rehearsal, 26, 32, 112–19, 145–57, 165–85, 189–98

Relaxation techniques, 42–43, 65–66,